Feasting
and Fasting

Feasting and Fasting

Canada's Heritage Celebrations

Dorothy Duncan

DUNDURN PRESS
TORONTO

Editor: Michael Carroll
Design: Jennifer Scott
Printer: Friesens

Library and Archives Canada Cataloguing in Publication

Duncan, Dorothy
    Feasting and fasting : Canada's heritage celebrations / by Dorothy Duncan.

Also issued in electronic format.
ISBN 978-1-55488-757-6

1. Fasts and feasts--Canada--History.   2. Food habits--Canada--History.   3. Holiday cookery--Canada--History.   I. Title.

TX739.D85 2010   641.5'68   C2010-902431-1

1   2   3   4   5   14   13   12   11   10

We acknowledge the support of the **Canada Council for the Arts** and the **Ontario Arts Council** for our publishing program. We also acknowledge the financial support of the **Government of Canada** through the **Canada Book Fund** and **The Association for the Export of Canadian Books**, and the **Government of Ontario** through the **Ontario Book Publishers Tax Credit** program, and the **Ontario Media Development Corporation.**

Care has been taken to trace the ownership of copyright material used in this book. The author and the publisher welcome any information enabling them to rectify any references or credits in subsequent editions.

J. Kirk Howard, President

Printed and bound in Canada.
www.dundurn.com

Dundurn Press
3 Church Street, Suite 500
Toronto, Ontario, Canada
M5E 1M2

Gazelle Book Services Limited
White Cross Mills
High Town, Lancaster, England
LA1 4XS

Dundurn Press
2250 Military Road
Tonawanda, NY
U.S.A. 14150

For my mother,
Margaret Ellen Gibson,
and
my maternal grandmother,
Georgina Murdoch Gibson,
with love and
gratitude

Contents

Acknowledgements

I would like to express my appreciation to all those who have contributed to this book and the stories it has to tell. Family, friends, neighbours, colleagues, and often total strangers have generously shared information, research, comments, criticism, and clues for further investigation.

First of all, a very special thanks to those dedicated individuals who actually made the publication happen in a timely manner: Colin Agnew for his constant support, advice, and attention to detail as the manuscript unfolded; and the staff of Dundurn Press for their expertise, knowledge, and patience, particularly Kirk Howard, Beth Bruder, Michael Carroll, and Jennifer Scott.

Those who made invaluable contributions include Jeanine Avigdor, York Pioneer and Historical Society; Jane Beecroft,

Community History Project and Tollkeeper's Cottage; Dr. Carl Benn, Ryerson University; Donald Booth, U.E., Toronto; Arthur Bousfield, Canadian Royal Heritage Trust; Dorette Carter, Art Gallery of Northumberland, Cobourg, Ontario; Dr. John Carter, Toronto; Janet Cobban, John R. Park Homestead, Essex County, Ontario; Nettie Cronish, president of the Women's Culinary Network; Eleanor Darke, Watford, Ontario; Paul Delaney, Penetanguishene, Ontario; Diabo, Kahnawke, Mohawk Territory; Dr. Victoria Dickenson, McCord Museum, Montreal, now Canadian Museum for Human Rights, Winnipeg; Naomi Duguid, Toronto; Judith and John Fitzhenry, Toronto; Dr. Rae Fleming, Argyle, Ontario; James Fortin, City of Greater Sudbury Heritage Museums; Mary Lou Fox, Ojibwa First Nation, Manitoulin Island; Jeanne Hopkins, Willowdale, Ontario; Alison Hughes, Richmond Hill; Jeanne Hughes, Richmond Hill; Lynne Jeffrey, Toronto; George Kapelos, Toronto; Ruth Keene, Willowdale; Linda Kelly, Sheguiandah, Manitoulin Island; Carolyn King, Mississaugas of the New Credit First Nation; Rosemary Kovac, Don Mills, Ontario; Robert Leverty, Ontario Historical Society; Joyce Lewis, Toronto; Lynn Lockhart, Orillia Public Library; Valerie Mah, Toronto; Mgizi-Kwe, Mnjikaning First Nation; Mariposa Writers' Group, Orillia, Ontario; Allan McGillivray, Zephyr, Ontario; Judith McGonigal, Sault Ste. Marie, Ontario; Micheline Mongrain-Dontigny, Saint-Irénée, Quebec; Nozhem, Mushkeego Anishnawabe First Nation;

Acknowledgements

Joyce Pettigrew, Otterville, Ontario; Josie and Keith Penny, Dunnville, Ontario; Dennis Pollock, Beaverton, Ontario; Joan and Donald Rumgay, Port Hope, Ontario; Nancy Scott, Sault Ste. Marie; Barbara Seargeant, Port Hope; Mary Simmonds, Whitby, Ontario; David Teitel, Toronto; Chris Tomasini and Kim Vallee, Lakehead University Library (Orillia Campus); Glenn Truax, Medicine Hat, Alberta; Inez and Winston Vokey, Barrie, Ontario; Ian Wheal, Toronto; and Nancy and Rod Williams, Orillia.

A very special word of gratitude for their support to my daughters, Barbara Ellen Truax and Carol Heather Agnew, and their families. Thank you!

Preface

*F*easting and Fasting: Canada's Heritage Celebrations *is an introduction to the special days, holidays, and holy days of our ancestors. For thousands of years before the arrival of newcomers to this land we call Canada, the First Nations were celebrating their passages of life, the changing seasons, and the gifts of food from the Great Spirit. They were guided by the sun and the moon as they recognized and honoured the circle of life that influenced their families, clans, and nations.*

As people from other continents arrived, they brought memories of celebrations in their homelands. Many had begun as pagan festivals, but as Christianity gained in popularity they were adopted into the Christian calendar. When Christianity moved out of its Mediterranean homeland, it encountered new folk traditions, leading to a fusion of cultural celebrations that made the process of transformation even more complex. After the newcomers encountered the First Nations, they recognized how similar some of the traditions were and how different others appeared to be.

Each new cultural group was accustomed to a calendar — Gregorian for the majority of Western Europe, Julian for some Eastern Europeans, lunar for some from Asia, and a combination of lunar and solar for people of Jewish ancestry. Thus one of the oldest and most universally celebrated events, New Year, has been and still is observed at various times in Canada. The different calendars mean that the date upon which a special day is observed may vary from year to year.

Even within a small community of neighbours, a diverse number of special days marking the passages of life, anniversaries, and religious occasions could be celebrated in sundry ways. William Lyon Mackenzie, recently arrived from Scotland in 1820 and later to become the first mayor of Toronto in 1834 and leader of the 1837 Rebellion, provides a glimpse of the complexity of cultures when he describes an election crowd in Niagara in Upper Canada (Ontario) in 1824:

> Christians, Heathens, Mennonites and Tunkards, Quakers and Universalists, Presbyterians and Baptists, Roman Catholics and American Methodists; there were Frenchmen and Yankees, Irishmen and Mulattoes,

Scotchmen and Indians, Englishmen, Canadians, Americans and Negroes, Dutchmen
and Germans, Welshmen and Swedes, Highlanders and Lowlanders, poetical as well as the
most prosaical phises, horsemen and footmen,
fiddlers and dancers, honourables and rever-
ends, captains and colonels, beaux and belles,
wagons and bilburies, coaches and chaises,
gigs and carts; in short Europe, Asia, Africa
and America had there each its representative
among the loyal subjects and servants of our
good King George, the fourth of the name.[1]

Despite their differences, newcomers wanted to fit in and
to become accepted by those already here, whether they were
French, English, Scottish, Irish, or Welsh. A spirit of hospitality in which people work and celebrate together dates back to
the First Nations who helped the initial settlers survive the
harsh conditions of the New World. They taught the newcomers about herbal remedies, introduced them to crane berries
(cranberries) and other unfamiliar flora and fauna, showed
them the art of tapping maple trees, and acted as guides and
advisers as colonists pushed farther into the forests to carve
out homesteads and build communities. Everyone had strong
ties to the land, the water, and what could be harvested, knowing there would be years of plenty and years of drought.

This way of life was based on the hard work, persistence, teamwork, and faith that bound communities together. Armed with only a few staple ingredients but possessing a great deal of ingenuity, these settlers from dissimilar backgrounds blended customs, traditions, and cultures and emerged with open doors, warm kitchens, hearty meals, and tasty desserts. They may have known, or had heard about, the lavish celebrations "at home," but in their new surroundings they celebrated not only the special days but their freedom and independence and recognized that they were masters of their own destinies at last.

Feasting and Fasting introduces not only everyday fare, but also the traditions and memories in Canada that revolved around food until about 1950. But why stop then?

The Dominion of Canada was born on July 1, 1867, after the passing of the British North America Act, which unified the colonies of Nova Scotia, New Brunswick, and the United Province of Canada (the name for the union of Upper and Lower Canada after 1841). However, Canada wasn't considered a nation yet, and it wasn't until the First World War that progress toward that goal was accomplished. All the British dominions made such valuable contributions during the war in support of the Mother Country that common interests and sentiments developed.[2]

On December 11, 1931, the Statute of Westminster was passed by the British Parliament, granting Canada and the other dominions full legal rights to independent national status. Canada had come of age!

Preface

Eight years later, though, Canada found itself in a second world war. During this conflict, Canadians truly matured into full nationhood. We trained men and women from around the world in Canada, and Canadian men and women served in countries globally, giving us all a deeper understanding of international goodwill.

Not long after the end of the war in 1945, we welcomed Newfoundland and Labrador as new members of the family. More than a million immigrants from more than forty countries called Canada their home in the next decade, bringing with them their skills, work ethics, ideas, crafts, music, art, food traditions, and celebrations. That is an enormous, unique, and exciting story and deserves its own place in our history, as well. But that is another story for another day.

Dorothy Duncan
Orillia, Ontario
October 2010

1

In the Beginning

"Let us abide with the ancients tonight!" exclaims the elder.
"Be it well," reply the listeners.

— "The Serpent of the Sea," *American Myths and Legends*

From the beginning of time the First Nations have been commemorating the passages of life, the changing of seasons, the sowing of seeds, the harvesting of crops, and many other events. Long before the arrival of newcomers, there were well-established traditions of feasting and fasting and celebrations that were as complex as the customs the newcomers brought with them. The First Nations' rituals have been recounted through the centuries by their elders and storytellers. In addition we have some written accounts by the newcomers that help us to understand the complexity of cultures, lifestyles, traditions, languages, and foodways that were, and continue to be, as different among Natives as among the newcomers themselves.

That rich history deserves its own volume, or series of volumes, to be recounted and recorded by the First Nations. Brief passages in several upcoming chapters weave parts of those traditions into the newcomers' stories. Elder Mary Lou Fox of the Ojibwa First Nation on Manitoulin Island was a wonderful teacher who shared her people's history and culture at every opportunity. Here she speaks about the Naming Ceremony:

> Things are done in a circle, and there's a lot of preparation. There's a lady now who's preparing in West Bay for her name, and also preparing for the name of her grandchild. These two names will be given and she has given tobacco to someone who's going to come up with the names, but she's been preparing for over a year as there's different things that you have to do. For instance, right now she's collecting blueberries that will be served at the feast. She has already collected raspberries. You have a giveaway, so she and her family have to make gifts for certain people that are

there and usually a gift is made for everybody. It's a lot of preparation to get a name. If it's a baby, then the family has to prepare the gifts, the foods, give tobacco and so on. You don't know what the name is going to be, only the person who's been given the responsibility. When you have everybody there, then your name is announced.

You have someone who's a master of ceremonies who orchestrates everything — where people are going to sit, how it's going to go and so on. Usually it starts off with a teaching. Just as an example, with the medicine wheel I said, "one of the teachings is that nothing may be done that will harm the children."

You've got the people in the circle, where an altar has been prepared. On a blanket you would have the pipe, the medicine wheel and sweetgrass [for some First Nations, sweetgrass is strictly a male medicine; for a female participant, sage is used instead]. You'd also have all the gifts that the family had made so those are all there too. All the gifts are blessed with the sweetgrass and the person who is giving the name invites the person who is going to get the name to come up, and only then is the name announced. Nobody knows what the name is until that moment so the name-giver will take that person and they will yell out the name. They say it to the universe so that everybody knows, and then the people who are attending are also asked to yell out the name to the four directions to the Creator. The name is yelled out four times and everybody faces the four directions. It starts with the east and the person is faced to the east; and everybody stands up and faces east and the name is yelled out then everybody yells the name out. That's done to the four directions. Then the person who is giving the name will talk about the name and they will say this is the name I chose, and this is why I chose the name, so the name-giver will explain all of that....

The one who receives the name is also invited to say something. This is the first time that person will talk about their identity with the new name. He'll talk about how he feels, he'll repeat his name so that he'll be comfortable with it, and the sponsors also will talk about their commitment and responsibilities. Then everybody comes up and shakes hands or gives a hug or a hug and kiss and shakes hands, and they say the name as they embrace or shake hands with the person. The name is being said often; people saying this is your identity, this is your name and it's important for you do these things. During this time, the food is in the circle, but it's not covered. The food is blessed and then after, there's a food offering where you take a little bit of food on a plate and it's offered to the spirits who have gone before us. It's either burned or is taken to a part in the bush that's nice and clean and left there for the Spirit.

The food is served in different ways depending on the ceremony that you're doing. At some ceremonies, it's the young men who will serve everybody, or it's the immediate family who prepare the food and then serve. There's also an order for serving the food: first would be the one who gave the name, then the sponsors, the elders, and the family eats the last. There's also food to be given away....

After you eat, you have a giveaway.... It's usually handmade stuff; you don't go out and buy stuff but spend the whole year preparing and making stuff especially for the name-giver and sponsors. It's special things like tobacco pouches or medicine wheel blankets, so you give from your heart.

The final step is singing a song, or saying a prayer, or both, because when you open something then it also must be closed. If you are using a pipe and it has been filled, then it must be smoked and cleaned and put away so then everything is closed. Finally, everyone comes up and shakes hands or hugs and kisses the person and says their name at the same time.[1]

The powwow is possibly the best-known Native celebration across Canada. Some of them were, and are, private celebrations, while others welcome the public. Powwows can be held for many reasons. For example, when the sugar moon appears, families move to maple groves "to open up the trees." They bring baskets of food for the feast, and after prayers of thanksgiving and ceremonial drinking of the sap, the tapping begins.

Perhaps the potlatch became one of the better known First Nations celebrations to new arrivals in western Canada. It is also known as the "donation" feast or the "giveaway dance or festival." *A Concise Dictionary of Canadianisms* tells us that: "Although the potlatch was most highly developed among the Kwakiutl of British Columbia, it played in one form or another, an important part in the culture of the Indians of the Pacific Coast from Oregon to Alaska and of those in the Interior of B.C. and the Northwest. The practice was outlawed in 1884 by the Potlatch Law."[2] The Potlatch Law remained on the statutes of Canada from April 19, 1884, until the Indian Act was revised completely in 1951.

A potlatch is held for many reasons: a young person assuming a new name, the construction of a new home, or the erection of a giant pole (called a crest or totem pole) in front of a home as the genealogical record of a family to confirm its status and position in the community. After a sumptuous feast, the host presents lavish gifts to the guests with the expectation that they will reciprocate at potlatches of their own. This competitive feasting is a source of great status for the participants and can lead to individuals attempting larger and more elaborate feasts and gifts, hoping to outdo the other members of their community.

2

Welcome to the New Year:
From Feast to Fast to Feast

*In the New Year, may your right hand always be
stretched out in friendship, never in want.*

— Irish Toast

*New Year's Day: Now is the accepted time to make
your regular annual good resolutions. Next week you
can begin paving hell with them as usual.*

— Mark Twain, Letter to
Virginia City Territorial Enterprise

As many Canadians celebrate New Year's Day on
January 1, we are continuing a tradition that began
in Roman times. Most of the ancient civilizations

celebrated the New Year with the coming of spring. The early Romans did, too, welcoming the New Year in March, close to the spring equinox. It was Julius Caesar who changed the Roman New Year's Day from March to January in honour of Janus, the god of all beginnings, the god of agriculture, and the keeper of the gates of heaven and earth. To mark the start of the New Year, Caesar decreed that the first month of the year was to be named after Janus and the first day of the month was to be dedicated to the Festival of Janus. Gifts were exchanged among friends, and resolutions of friendship and love to one another were made. The entire day was given over to festivities.

When the Romans under Constantine the Great accepted Christianity as their new faith, they kept the Festival of Janus as their New Year's Day. In the seventeenth century, Scottish Presbyterians allied with English Puritans to suppress the festivals of Christmas and the New Year. The latter feast day was turned into a fast and a day of prayer to be spent in solemn meditation, repentance, making good resolutions, and turning over a new leaf to mark the death of the old year and the rebirth of the new.[1]

About three centuries ago a change again took place as Christians slowly transformed New Year's Day back to a happy, joyful time of celebration and observed the beliefs, superstitions, and customs they hoped would bring them good fortune in the New Year. These included notions such as: if you fed hens all the fruit in the house, they would lay well for the next twelve months; if you swept floors on this day, they would cause the death of someone who lived in the house; and many, many more!

If you wanted to know if you were going to have a good year, you consulted the Bible, the font of truth, to foretell the future. It was opened at a random page on New Year's morning, and with eyes closed, a pin was stuck in the page. The verse predicted the good or evil nature of the ensuing twelve months.

The above are just a few of the beliefs and traditions that arrived in Canada along with the newcomers. They also brought with them the memories of traditional foods they had enjoyed on this day:

> On New Year's morning it was the Québécois custom for the eldest son to ask his father for his blessing. Later in the day, French Canadian families tried to gather together under the roof of the oldest member for a special dinner. Dried apple pie was a traditional specialty. After dinner families attended mass together.[2]

When families gather on New Year's for a hearty meal, a favourite or traditional specialty is usually on the table. These can differ dramatically as two examples illustrate. The Acadians, who began settling in eastern Canada in the late seventeenth century, favoured Poutine Râpées made from raw and cooked potatoes, onions, and either fresh lean pork or salted fat pork, while Greek settlers who arrived in Manitoba in the late nineteenth century baked Vasilopeta or Basilopita, their New Year's bread in honour of St. Basil, whose feast is celebrated on January 1. To this day, Greek Canadians continue the tradition: a coin is baked into the bread and whoever receives that slice will have good luck in the New Year.

The custom of exchanging gifts on New Year's Day was well established in France and other European countries. In England the monarch announced that gifts were welcome on this day, and "Queen Elizabeth I of England often found her royal warehouses bulging with gifts of every kind after January 1."[3]

While the giving or exchanging of gifts didn't become popular in Canada, the custom of paying New Year's calls on the ladies in the community by gentlemen of French, English, or Scottish ancestry certainly did. This was an excellent opportunity for unmarried men to call on unmarried women, since in a very short time they could meet many eligible girls. Refreshments were laid out for the gentlemen and could range from wine and cake, to sherry and Christmas cake, to sandwiches, cookies, and fruitcake, with freshly brewed tea and coffee. From the *Diary* of Elizabeth Russell, sister of Peter Russell, the administrator of Upper Canada, we have a description of these calls in York (now Toronto), Upper Canada:

Janry 1st, 1806

Wednesday. When I came to breakfast found
Dr. Baldwin. He wished the compts of the
Season — St. George was here before I was
up — Miss Sheehan came while at breakfast,
and took a dish of chocolate … After chatting
some time she went away. After she was gone
came Mr. Ridout, then Mr. Saml Ridout, and
both went away together. Then came Lucy
Slegman with little Robert [Baldwin] — then
young Small, then his father who came up to
me to wish the compts of the Season. Made
a distant curtsy. He did not take my hand or
salute [a chaste kiss]. He gave Robert an apple.
His son & he went away together — Robert
did not stay much longer … St. George came
before dinner — then came Willcocks who
dined with us, Denison came in at dinner
time & he & Willcocks stayed the evening.[4]

This type of hospitality was long and perhaps tiring, but
in the formal traditions of the community it was essential for
the hostess and visiting gentlemen because it allowed them to
uphold the upper-class traditions of their homelands.

New Year's Day was also the opportunity for clergy and government leaders such as mayors, reeves, and heads of state to host levees or receptions. Lieutenant-Colonel R.B. McCrea (Robert Barlow) of the Royal Artillery shares his experience as he pays four visits on New Year's 1869 in St. John's, Newfoundland. In this account, perhaps, we find a subtle way for the hosts to refresh themselves during the long and tedious reception:

> Crossing too over the chequered marble in the hall of Government House, in our visit to the venerable chieftain who, in his red morocco chair of state looked like one of the Northern Vikings … "Thank ye, thank ye, gentlemen said he as we offered our congratulations … I am just treating this confounded cough with a little plain water, and a squeeze of orange in it" … We soon found ourselves under the portico of his honour the Chief-Justice. Like his best friend the Governor, Sir Francis whispered, "Be off with your blarney, and get a glass of something with Lady Brady. I've a bad cough, and I'm just moistening my throat with a little water, with a squeeze of orange in it." … When we stood in the parlour of the jolly old President of the Council he should remark — "And what will ye be taken, mee

three dear fellows? Is it poort? You see I'm just moistening mee lips with a drop of water, with a squeeze of orange in it; help yourselves: ... Our last visit was to *the* great man: ... the Bishop stood — about to receive the address of congratulation from the "Sons of Fishermen" or the Irish Society ... We paid our respects and congratulations as was right and proper. A hearty reciprocation and a glass of champagne were his return for the compliment.[5]

The tradition of families gathering for a hearty meal as the New Year begins has been and continues to be popular in many parts of Canada. Here is a simple menu that has stood the test of time and popularity:

NEW YEAR'S DAY DINNER

Traditional Roast Beef
Horse-radish Sauce
Yorkshire Pudding
Potatoes and Onions
(browned with the meat)
Mincemeat Pie
Fruit Cake

Coffee   Milk[6]

3

Sir John A. at Table

J ohn Alexander Macdonald was born in Glasgow, Scotland,
on January 10 or 11, 1815, the eldest son of a struggling
businessman, Hugh Macdonald, and his wife, Helen Shaw.
Glasgow at that time, like so many other cities in Scotland
and England, was struggling to survive cycles of recession,
resulting in jobless citizens, and a series of epidemics. Bleak

prospects for the future forced many Scots, including the Macdonalds, to immigrate to British North America.

The family took passage on the *Earl of Buckinghamshire*, and after a forty-two-day voyage arrived in Quebec in June 1820. They settled first in Kingston, a bustling town with a population of about three thousand, and later in the Hay Bay, Adolphustown area of the Bay of Quinte. John walked about three miles every day to the local one-room schoolhouse. Later he attended Midland District Grammar School and Maxwell Academy.

His home, like so many other Scottish ones, would have been frugal. The cost of supplies at that time would have been expensive for them: a barrel of flour $2, a bushel of potatoes or a loaf of sugar 1 shilling each, a pound of maple sugar 4 pence, cheese 6 pence, pork or butter 3 pence each. So the Macdonalds would have planted a garden and bought a cow and fowls as soon as possible, while father Hugh supported his family first as a shopkeeper and later as a miller. Mother Helen would have brought with her memories of their favourite foods on the table in Glasgow, and with limited resources but great inventiveness, she attempted to continue the traditions of Oatmeal Porridge, Oatmeal Bread, Oatcakes, Bannock, Barley Broth, Nettle Soup, Haggis, Clapshot or Neeps and Tatties (boiled and mashed turnips and potatoes), honey, orange marmalade, Scottish Trifle, Black Bun, and Scotch Shortbread washed down with strong lashings of tea at their table in Canada.

John left school at age fifteen to earn his living by studying law and articling to George Mackenzie, a prominent lawyer in Kingston. In 1834 when Mackenzie died during a cholera epidemic that killed twelve hundred of his fellow citizens, John took over the practice and was called to the bar a few years later.

Macdonald was a young man who was very proud of his Scottish heritage and had been one of the organizers of the St. Andrew's Society in Kingston, serving as its president and learning to play the bagpipes. Later he became a proud member of the Order of Ancient Free and Accepted Masons of Canada.

When the Imperial Act of Union transformed Upper and Lower Canada into the new Province of Canada, Kingston was named the capital on February 6, 1841. This development, of course, delighted the residents, but sadly that year John's beloved and easygoing father, Hugh, passed away. Soon after his father's death, John himself became quite ill, probably due to a combination of grief and overwork, and was persuaded to visit England and Scotland. With his love of the traditions of his ancestors and his homeland, it might not have been too difficult for him to accept that the sea voyage and a change in scenery would have a healing effect. He not only regained his health but also fell in love with his cousin Isabella, daughter of Captain William Clark of Dalnavert, Scotland, and they were married on September 1, 1843, in St. Andrew's Presbyterian Church in Kingston.

John served briefly as an alderman in Kingston before being elected to the Parliament of Upper Canada in 1844, representing the Kingston Conservatives. By now the capital had moved to Montreal, and John travelled to the new Parliament House at St. Anne's Market to take his place in the Provincial Legislature.

This was the beginning of a political career for a man whose parents had fled the poverty and pestilence of their homeland to seek a new life in a new country. No one could have visualized that Hugh's son, the "wee baron" John, just five years old when he left Scotland, would have such a powerful effect on the future moulding and defining of that new nation.

Macdonald was elected prime minister of the Province of Canada in November 1857, but this public honour was overshadowed by personal loss when Isabella died a few weeks later. His public life had now become a hectic round of meetings, entertaining, being entertained, and formal banquets. One example was in 1860 when John hosted eight hundred guests at a magnificent St. Valentine's Day Ball on February 14 in the Music Hall of the St. Louis Hotel in Quebec City.[1] Edward, Prince of Wales, also made his first royal visit to Canada in 1860, and in his official capacity John was prominent at the dinners, teas, balls, receptions, and other social events designed to welcome and honour Queen Victoria's son and heir.

The 1860s were a turbulent decade for John, with political upheavals, proposals, and counterproposals as the four provinces of Nova Scotia, New Brunswick, Prince Edward Island, and Canada met and explored confederation at their now-famous meetings in the shady village of Charlottetown in September 1864. We learn from the newspapers of the day — *Ross's Weekly* or the *Protestant* — that it wasn't all dry speeches, debates, and compromises, and this notion is confirmed by Harry Bruce in *Canada 1812–1871: The Formative Years*:

> Yes, those same stiff-necked characters in the famous portrait ... those fellows with the mutton-chop whiskers and the dark, heavy, discreet narrow-legged woolen suits ... with their cheeks full of potatoes and their apparently glum, Victorian, Sunday-morning faces ... those same men, the whole rollicking bunch of them, stayed up all through the night of September 7–8, 1864, at the Grand Ball at Province House in Charlottetown.
>
> They arrived at 10, and they danced the local women around the hall, and they boozed it up, and they made florid speeches, and they didn't even start to eat till one in the morning. Then, somewhere around 5 a.m., they all made their way down through the warm island fog to the harbour and climbed

aboard the steamship *Queen Victoria* for a
trip to Nova Scotia.

There they would continue their "delib-
erations." They were founding a nation, and
all through that astonishing, euphoric and frequently comic summer and autumn of 1864
they were proving that man does not found a
nation on bread alone.[2]

By 1865, Saint John's *Weekly Telegraph* was crudely describing the historic Charlottetown and Quebec conferences as
"the great intercolonial drunk of last year." The *Perth Courier*
referred to Confederation as "the measure of the Quebec ballroom and the oyster-supper statesmen," and even while the
Quebec Conference was still underway, the *Berliner Journal*
was so bold as to suggest that, no matter what the delegates
did on their forthcoming trip to Canada West, they couldn't
possibly expect any worse hangovers than they had already
acquired.[3] Hangovers aside, it is obvious there was far more
warmth, passion, intemperance, and colour to the founding
of Canada than one would expect from this Victorian colony.

Despite the press, they were successful. On July 1, 1867,
the passing of the British North America Act in Great Britain
led to the formation of the Dominion of Canada, with Ottawa
chosen by Queen Victoria as its capital. There was general
consensus that John, with his directing mind and moulding

hand, was the leading statesman, and he had the honour of being called upon to be the first prime minister of Canada and was knighted by Queen Victoria in June 1867.

During this period, political picnics came into vogue whenever an election loomed. It is believed that the first political picnic in Canada was held in Uxbridge, Ontario, in 1876, followed by hundreds more across the country sponsored by John A. and the Conservatives. An estimated five hundred guests attended that first picnic, and between political speeches by Sir John, Charles Tupper, Matthew Crooks Cameron, and William McDougall, they consumed the delectable provisions prepared by the ladies.[4] Little wonder that his opponents said: "If John A's stomach holds out, we will stay out."[5]

As Sir John became more famous, his name appeared in some unexpected places. For instance, the *Daily Telegraph* in Saint John, New Brunswick, notes his presence on December 21, 1878:

CHRISTMAS NOTES OF THE CITY MARKET

Yesterday the City Market contained a large quantity of country produce. The sales were heavy, and towards evening the quantity on hand was quite stinted. The season this year commences earlier than it did last year, but sales are not quite so brisk. However, they will, no doubt, be much larger than last year's transactions, as business will be much accelerated on the near approach of Christmas. The most noticeable feature in the building is the display of beef and poultry, which are specially fed and prepared for the Christmas holidays.

O'NEILL BROS.

Stall No. 5, on the north side of the market, is occupied by the above named firm. They have in their stall a pair of steers which weighed 2625 lbs.; another, 2080; another, 1780; and the sides of a young pair of cattle, fresh, clear and nicely coloured, gave a weight of 1000 pounds. Messers. O'Neill have also 500 turkey, geese, etc., all fine looking birds. Several have been labelled, and one magnificent turkey carcass weighing 23 pounds is christened the "Beaconsfield"; the "Marquis of Lorne" rolls up 20 pounds, and "Sir John A. Macdonald" 18½ pounds.[6]

Typical of Sir John's busy life was the Junior Conservative Club Banquet in the Windsor Hotel in Montreal on January 13, 1885, in honour of his birthday[7]:

JUNIOR CONSERVATIVE CLUB

2194.1

BANQUET

TO THE

Rt. Hon. SIR JOHN A. MacDONALD G. C. B.

WINDSOR HOTEL, MONTREAL,

January 13th 1885.

LIST * OF * TOASTS.

PROPOSED BY   RESPONSE BY.

THE QUEEN.

Mr. JOHN S. HALL Jr., Chairman

THE GOVERNOR GENERAL.

THE CHAIRMAN.

ARMY, NAVY & VOLUNTEERS.

Mr. R. D. McGIBBON.   HON. A. P. CARON,

OUR GUEST.

The Right Hon. SIR JOHN A, MacDONALD, G.C.B.
THE CHAIRMAN.

THE CABINET OF THE DOMINION.

Mr. C J. DOHERTY,   Hon. SIR HECTOR LANGEVIN, K.C.M.G.
1st Vice President J. C.C.
              Hon. SIR LEONARD TILLEY, K. C. M. G.

THE PARLIAMENT OF CANADA.

Mr. C. P. DAVIDSON, Q. C.   Hon. SIR DAVID McPHERSON K.C.M.G.
          Hon. J. A. CHAPLEAU,   Hon. JOHN COSTIGAN.

THE PROVINCIAL LEGISLATURES.

Mr. J. L. ARCHAMBAULT.   Hon. J. J. ROSS, Premier of Quebec.
       Hon. W. W. LYNCH,   Mr. W. R. MEREDITH, ONT.
         Hon. JOHN NORQUAY, MAN.

AGRICULTURE, COMMERCE & MANUFACTURES.

Mr. D. A. MacMASTER, Q. C., M. P.   G. A. DRUMMOND.
         Hon. LOUIS BEAUBIEN, M. P. P.
         Mr. HUGH McLENNAN. M. G. BOIVIN.

THE PRESS.

Mr. J. PHILIP WITHERS.

THE LADIES.

Mr. F. C. HENSHAW.   Mr. J. G. H. BERGERON, M.P,
         Mr. J. deH. FENWICK.

GOD SAVE THE QUEEN.

S. ENGLISH & CO.

With Sir John A. Macdonald's unexpected death on June 6, 1891, the tradition of recognizing and honouring him on or near his birthday with a gala dinner has continued in many communities in Canada. They are often sponsored by political organizations or history and heritage societies and feature good food, good fellowship, and a toast to the man many Canadians believe was "the leading Father of Confederation."

4

Remembering "Rabbie" Burns

O my Luve's like a red, red rose
That's newly sprung in June;
O my Luve's like the melodie
That's sweetly play'd in tune.

— Robert Burns, "A Red, Red Rose"

Wee "Rabbie" Burns was born in a two-room cottage in Alloway, a village outside Ayr, Scotland, on January 25, 1759. His parents, Agnes and William Burns, leased seven acres as a market garden and were concerned that Rabbie and his brother, Gilbert, receive an education and not remain farmers forever.

Robbie, or Robert, as he became known as he grew older, began writing poetry, ballads, and songs based on the life he knew — humble verses describing everyday life and the trials, tribulations, joys, and sorrows of his friends, family, and neighbours. The land, friendship, love, food, animals, birds, drink, and amusement were all topics that he explored with the language of his heart.

Burns's father died in 1784, an exhausted and bankrupt man who had been dogged by ill luck all his life. Two years later, in July 1786, Robbie managed to publish his first book of poetry, which was an instant success. He was accepted as a Freemason by St. David's (later St. James') Lodge in Tarbolton, and it wasn't long before the plowman-poet was welcomed by Edinburgh society.

Robbie eventually found steady employment as an excise tax collector for the British government. He often covered two hundred miles a week on horseback in all types of weather, and of course had to provide his own horse. Robbie earned £50 yearly, one half of the goods he seized, and £50 for every arrested smuggler.

Burns married Jean Armour and is alleged to have had several other liaisons, as well, and fathered thirteen children before his untimely death in 1796 at age thirty-seven. Ten thousand people joined the funeral procession to St. Michael's Kirkyard in Dumfries where he was buried.

Why did new arrivals from Scotland continue the tradition

of honouring Robbie Burns in Canada? The Scotland that Burns knew and wrote about, and the Edinburgh that received him so warmly, was the landscape and streetscape well-known to many of the original Scottish fur traders, Montreal merchants, and later settlers who came in that great wave of immigration in the late eighteenth and early nineteenth century. There was a growing recognition of Scottish pride, self-consciousness, and identity that was emphasized in Burns's poems, songs, and ballads. The immigrants to Canada would also have known that "back home" in Scotland the custom of an annual Burns Supper had already begun in Greenock in 1801. The newly formed St. Andrew's and Caledonian societies in Canada were intent on developing a firm infrastructure for immigrant Scottish communities, and this traditional annual supper and celebration of a beloved Scottish son became firmly established.

Much of Burns's poetry idolized the humble food and beverages of his homeland, and it was logical that the meal celebrating him reflected the meals he loved, as well as the meals the newcomers had known since birth. The "Selkirk Grace" was the traditional blessing of the meal:

> Some hae meat, and canna eat,
> And some wad eat that want it;
> But we hae meat and we can eat,
> And sae the Lord be thankit.[1]

Although Burns wrote many other graces, the one on the previous page endured.

For homesick newcomers, the fellowship of sharing a meal of Haggis and hearing Burns's "Address to a Haggis," along with Cock-a-Leekie Soup, Roast Beef with Horseradish Sauce, Neeps and Tatties (turnips and potatoes), and Scottish Trifle laced with Scotch whisky, was irresistible. The piping in of the Haggis, that "great chieftain o' the puddin' race!" at any feast in the early days saw Scottish gentlemen leaping onto their chairs, putting a foot on the table, and tossing back a glass of whisky. They would then toss their wineglasses onto the floor or into the fireplace.

As the years passed, the tradition didn't disappear but became more restrained. There would still be a piper to bring tears to their eyes as the guests raised their glasses to toast not only Burns and the Haggis but the homeland and absent brethren, as well.

Haggis became the national dish of Scotland, holding a place of honour not only on Robbie Burns's birthday but on Hogmanay, St. Andrew's Day, and wherever and whenever Scots celebrated. What is there about Haggis that gives it a place of honour wherever Scots gather?

The Dictionary of Gastronomy tells us that the delights of Haggis mixtures were discovered thousands of years ago, possibly as soon as humans cooked meat and certainly by the time they developed the mixing of flour foods with it. Around 400

B.C. the ancient Greek playwright Aristophanes described the explosion of a "stuffed sheep's paunch" incautiously attacked at table.

English recipes for Haggis survive from the early fifteenth century, and it was a popular dish in England and continued to be until the eighteenth century. The traditional Scottish dish (usually of sheep's pluck) is a pudding or sausage boiled in the cleansed stomach bag of the animal.[2]

So it is this fat sausage that moved Robert Burns in the eighteenth century to compose his eight-verse long "Address to a Haggis," the grace that ends with the words "If you will grant Scotland's grateful prayers, give her a Haggis!"

For those who don't want to search for a sheep's stomach to make Haggis in the traditional way, a modern version called Pan Haggis is becoming popular with Scots around the world. It is a combination of boiled grated liver and onion, suet, oatmeal, salt, pepper, and herbs simmered or steamed until the flavours are well blended.

Burns's birthday grew in popularity across Canada for those of Scottish ancestry and all those who wished they were. It is January 25 — remember wee Rabbie Burns as you join and sing about that long-ago time that he called "Auld Lang Syne," written by him to the melody of an old Scottish folk tune.

On January 25, 1793, Burns heard a thrush singing on his morning walk on his thirty-fourth birthday and wrote in part:

Sing on, sweet thrush, upon the leafless bough,
Sing on, sweet bird, I listen to thy strain:
See aged Winter, 'mid his surly reign,
At thy blythe carol clears his furrowed brow.[3]

Generations of Canadians of Scottish ancestry have been doing just that wherever and whenever they celebrate the birth and hear the words, songs, and poems of wee Rabbie Burns as they feast on the foods he knew and loved.

5

L'Ordre de bon temps,
Order of Good Cheer

We passed this winter most joyously, & fared lavishly.

— Samuel de Champlain

Samuel de Champlain was born in the French seaport town of Bourage on the Bay of Biscay in 1567. Although he trained as a naval officer, he had seen much action on land and fought with distinction for his king in Brittany.

Champlain's adventurous spirit led him to make a hazardous voyage of discovery to the West Indies; he visited Panama and the principal islands, and despite the efforts of the jealous Spaniards to keep foreigners out, he managed to reach the city of Mexico. This eager explorer didn't hesitate when he was invited to join a small group of French merchants who had formed a company and received from King Henri IV of France a monopoly of the fur trade in the Gulf of St. Lawrence region. Sieur de Monts and Sieur Pontgravé, along with Champlain, were determined to establish a successful colony on the mainland north of the Spanish settlement.

In the early summer of 1604, they probed possible sites along the shores of Acadia, now present-day Nova Scotia. When the expedition rounded Cape Sable and entered St. Mary's Bay, a party landed to explore. A priest named Nicholas Aubry strolled off into the forest and became lost. When departure time arrived, his comrades were forced to leave without him. The ships continued their voyage until finally they chose Île Saint-Croix (now Dochet Island) at the mouth of the Saint Croix River for the site of the first Habitation.

All hands were soon at work, except for a small party that went back to St. Mary's Bay in search of gold and silver. As they neared the shore, they noticed a small black object set up on a pole and recognized it as the hat of Father Aubry, the lost priest! They soon found him starved and emaciated after sixteen days of solitude and involuntary fasting. The exploring party returned to St. Croix with their lost comrade to find dwellings, storehouses, a chapel, barracks, and a magazine rising in the form of a square. A great bake oven of burnt brick was built to supply the kitchen, and palisades surrounded the establishment.

This was a busy little community of seventy-nine men, the only European settlement in the vast continent north of the Spanish settlements. In their enthusiasm to construct the necessary buildings before winter, they cut down most of the trees, not realizing how valuable they would be as a windbreak and as fuel in the months ahead. Ice clogged the river, cutting them off from supplies of wood and water on the mainland. They were forced to eat their food raw and to dole out their frozen cider and wine measured by the pound. By spring, scurvy had carried off thirty-five men who were buried in the new cemetery beside the chapel. The decision was made to look for a new site. By July the move was underway across the Bay of Fundy to what became known as Port Royal in the Annapolis Basin. They moved everything possible — stores, tools, equipment, utensils, and even portions of buildings. This was a sheltered site, and hunting and fishing were good, but despite the improvements twelve more men died from scurvy during the winter of 1605–06.[1]

In the summer of 1606, Champlain organized the famous Order of Good Cheer (L'Ordre de bon temps) to produce a little variety in their solitary and monotonous life, which he believed was causing their deaths. The knights were fifteen in number, and a grand master or steward was appointed for each day, whose duty it was to provide for the table of the company. In order to do this credibly and add a new dish daily, the knights, in turn, worked energetically to supply the board partly by their own exertions in hunting and fishing, partly by bartering with First Nations people. By this means, the company feasted sumptuously each day.

Marc Lescarbot, a Parisian poet, playwright, and lawyer, gives us an account of some of the ingredients and dishes that were served: "good dishes of meat ... *colice*, a hearty broth made from a cock, white sausages made from the flesh and innards of cod with lard and spice, good pastries made of moose and turtledoves."[2] Great ceremony attended the evening meal as the steward

> did march with his napkin on his shoulder and his staff of office in his hand, with the collar of the order about his neck, which was worth above four crowns, and all of them of the order following him, bearing every one a dish. The like was also at the bringing in of the fruit, but not with so great a train. And at night after grace was said, he resigned the collar of the order, with a cup of wine to his successor in that charge, and they drank one to another.[3]

Despite the ravages of scurvy, Port Royal survived and became not only the site of the first successful colony on the mainland but also the location of Canada's first social club.

First Nations and newcomers feasted together at a table laden with a wide range of food choices as two later authors attest:

> In the days of the Order of the Good Cheer, the Indians who came to the feasts at the Habitation often chose to make their meal of bread. It was a novelty to the Micmacs who did not grow wheat and therefore never knew the taste of bread before the coming of the white man.[4]

> One of the popular dishes was a delightful seafood chowder. The seafood was gathered from the riches of the sea; the word *chowder* originated from the French *chaudière*, a type of pot in which it was made. The delectable taste of this simmering soup reminds us of this rich heritage and the bountiful harvest of seafood in the waters of Nova Scotia.[5]

6

St. Valentine and the Foods of Love

Somebody loves you, deep and true,
If I weren't so bashful, I'd tell you who!

— Anonymous

Who was St. Valentine? For close to two thousand years, historians have researched the life and death of not one but three men in the hope of finding the origins of this celebration. All three men were put to death between 269 and 271 A.D. — an obscure North African martyr; a Roman physician who converted to Christianity, became a priest, and was executed for performing marriages that the Roman Emperor Claudius II had forbidden;

and Bishop Valentinus of Terni (a diocese a few miles from Rome). Valentinus, too, was conducting prohibited marriages, and when arrested, attempted unsuccessfully to convert the emperor to Christianity and was put to death for his efforts. A legend tells us that, while in prison, Valentinus sent messages "From your Valentine" and "Your Valentine" to his jailor's daughter, whose sight he had restored.

The deaths of these martyrs occurred close to the date of Lupercalia, a popular pagan fertility festival. As Christianity grew in popularity, many pagan festivals were transformed and renamed to become Christian feasts, and suddenly the celebration of St. Valentine, the patron saint of lovers, emerged.

The tradition of giving gifts and cards with messages of friendship and love grew in popularity in the late Middle Ages as many believed that February 14 was the day that birds chose their mates, and therefore, all single folks should do the same. As Christianity and the celebration of St. Valentine spread across Europe to France and Great Britain, the custom of delivering messages of affection was often combined with food. In England a gentleman might toss an apple or an orange through the front door of his beloved's home with a romantic message tied to it and then disappear from her sight. The tradition continued to grow as William Shakespeare wrote about St. Valentine in *Hamlet*, with Ophelia saying, "Good morrow, 'tis St. Valentine's Day, / All in the morn betime, / And I a maid at your window, / to be your valentine."

Gentlemen such as the well-known English Admiralty official Samuel Pepys described the revelry of the day several times in his famous *Diary* between 1660 and 1669, with many references to the gifts the ladies expected from their suitors. White gloves were much coveted as gifts, since they were tied by tradition to courting and marriage ceremonies and signified a clean hand and a symbol of innocence.

English stationers began printing valentines commercially, and eager suitors swamped the mail carriers with these affectionate missives. New arrivals in Canada from England, Ireland, Scotland, and Wales would have known about the traditions and folklore that surrounded the day. In February 1877, English-born John Howard recorded in his diary that "he bought a valentine for his ill wife Jemima for the sum of $1.25." This at a time when her nurse was earning $2.50 a week! When Jemima died in September 1877, John included among her personal effects sent to her sister, Mrs. Mountcastle, in Clinton, Ontario, two valentines, a touching demonstration of the sentimentality and value attached to them.

Hand in hand with the tradition of exchanging letters, cards, and gifts was the growing belief that certain foods were aphrodisiacs and therefore important to courting a loved one. At one time or another practically every food in the world has fallen into this category because of its shape, nutritional qualities, colour, or the folklore surrounding it. This includes herbs such as ginseng and cyclamen, flowers, vegetables such as carrots, fresh or dried fruit, seafood (especially oysters), eggs, nuts, and spices.

There appears to be no scientific support for many of these beliefs, while others such as chocolate have venerable reputations. Chocolate and the cacao bean from which it derives have been renowned as aphrodisiacs for centuries, beginning with the Natives of Central America who served it to their bravest soldiers after successful battles and to their gods at important celebrations of births, marriages, and deaths.

The Aztec king Montezuma, who had a large harem, is purported to have sipped fifty golden goblets of this nectar every day to give him strength and energy. Casanova, one of the most accomplished lovers of all time, favoured chocolate over champagne to put him in a romantic mood. In the eighteenth century the Swedish scientist, naturalist, and physician Carolus Linnaeus gave the cacao tree the name "food of the gods," and the world's love affair with chocolate started in earnest.

In 1831, John Cadbury opened a chocolate business in England. His sons, George and Richard, formed a partnership and eventually took over the company. Thirty years later Richard Cadbury created the first St. Valentine's box of chocolate. Within a decade, chocolatiers in Canada were in business, with Mott's Chocolate Factory established in Dartmouth, Nova Scotia, in 1844. Their long sticks of chocolate sold in stores for a penny and soon became popular. The Ganong

Brothers began operating in St. Stephen, New Brunswick, in 1873, and Rogers' Chocolate was founded in Victoria, British Columbia, in 1885 by Charles (Candy) Rogers in the back of his small grocery store.

Sir John A. Macdonald may have hosted the most spectacular St. Valentine's Ball ever planned in Canada. One thousand tickets at a dollar each were sent out to invite his friends and supporters to join him in the Music Hall of the St. Louis Hotel in Quebec City on February 14, 1860. The ballroom was a spectacle of wonder, with garlands of roses, a bust of Her Majesty, Queen Victoria, the Palms of Edward, Prince of Wales, flags, a statue of Cupid, and a fountain of eau de cologne! John A. himself, a merry host, gallantly presented valentines "with pretty little remarks" to the ladies.

At the supper hour Macdonald delighted his guests again with an extremely large pie, out of which flew four and twenty birds! Supper, with a wide selection of delicacies served, cost him $520. The liquor consumed that evening included eleven dozen bottles of champagne, two dozen bottles of sparkling moselle, three dozen bottles of sherry, a dozen bottles of best port, six dozen bottles of Allsops Ale, and two dozen bottles of porter, for a cost of $1,086.70. Really, a very modest expenditure to delight the eight hundred guests who accepted his invitation.[1]

Over the years Canadians have continued to celebrate with enthusiasm on February 14, despite the mysterious origins of the day. Gifts, cards, tokens of affection, and romantic meals — breakfast, brunch, lunch, tea, or dinner — are still enjoyed in hotels, restaurants, and at home.

Our Canadian ancestors, whether First Nations or newcomers, have always been ingenious in the preparation of food as they have searched for roots, herbs, fruit, and other ingredients necessary to make love potions, gifts for loved ones, and foods for romantic encounters. For a simple repast with a special friend or your family, you may want to try one, or all, of these Canadian favourites that have stood the test of time:

OYSTERS

Oysters have long been considered the premier food of love, but unfortunately they were not easily available in many regions of Canada in the colonial period so recipes were developed by ingenious housewives to imitate this treasured but often elusive delicacy.

"How to make Mock Oysters out of Canadian Corn" appeared in handwritten cookery books and printed books in the nineteenth century:

Grate ½ dozen ears of corn with a coarse grater, beat the whites and yolks of 3 eggs, and add them to the corn, with 1 table-spoon flour, 1 tablespoon butter, 1 teaspoon salt and pepper to taste. Stir.well and drop spoonfuls of this batter into a frying pan with hot butter and lard and fry to a light brown on both sides.[2]

ST. VALENTINE PARFAIT

1 cup sugar
½ cup water
1 tablespoon vanilla
2 cups heavy cream
whites of 3 eggs
maraschino cherries

Boil sugar and water until syrup forms a thread, then pour it slowly over the stiffly beaten whites, stirring constantly. Cool this mixture thoroughly, then fold into whipped cream, flavour, and pile lightly into individual paper or silver freezing dishes. Garnish with maraschino cherries cut into small hearts, or sprinkle with decorative candy hearts. Freeze for 3 or 4 hours. This will serve 10 persons.[3]

FOOD FOR THE GODS

3 eggs
1 tablespoon milk
10 graham crackers rolled
1 cup brown sugar
2 teaspoons baking powder
1 cup chopped walnuts
1 cup dates

Beat eggs with milk. Add remaining ingredients and mix. Bake in greased pan in 350-degree oven for 30–40 minutes. When cool, spread with butter icing and top with chopped walnuts. Cut in squares.[4]

RUNAWAY CAKE

1 egg
1 teaspoon of sugar
1 cup of water
1 cup of milk
2 teaspoons of cream of tartar
1 teaspoon of soda

Flour to make a little thicker than griddle
cakes, then bake on a griddle and eat hot
with butter.[5]

The cake in the last recipe can certainly be produced in a
hurry, and the name conjures up intriguing visions of an elop-
ing couple hastily replenishing their strength before fleeing the
anger of their families.

St. Valentine's Day is a joyful feast, so to exchange, to serve,
and to enjoy confections seems most suitable on this day.

7

Gung Hei Fat Choi —
May You Have
Good Fortune and Riches!

Our lives are not in the lap of the gods, but in the lap of our cooks.

— Lin Yutang

Gold! Just one lucky strike, and an instant fortune was all that was needed to lure thousands of prospectors and miners to the goldfields of British Columbia in 1858. For a short time Canada was known as Gum San, the Land of Gold, or Golden Mountain, to the new arrivals from China who came to prospect for gold, work on construction projects, build new railways, and open their own businesses. Between 1881 and 1885, it is believed more than fifteen thousand Chinese immigrated to Canada, entering by one of the ports on the West Coast. Many of these new arrivals were strong, able-bodied men, and they were often referred to as bachelor societies. It wasn't until the twentieth century that Canadian immigration laws were relaxed and allowed the arrival of wives, sweethearts, and family members in growing numbers.

From modest beginnings, Canadians of Chinese ancestry have made incredible contributions to Canadian life and food-ways. They were among our first market gardeners and fisher-men who shipped food inland to those hungry gold miners. As their friends and colleagues helped construct the railways that eventually spanned the nation, many men travelled to eastern Canada, again to develop market gardens and green-houses or open restaurants and grocery stores.

Chinese districts began to emerge in provinces other than British Columbia. For example, in the early 1890s two Chinese men, Wing Lee and Chung Gee, arrived in Edmonton, Alberta, and opened laundries on Jasper Avenue. By 1899, Low's *Edmonton and District Directory* listed not only their laundries but also two Chinese restaurants nearby, where Edmonton's Chinatown eventually developed. These restaurants, and those that followed, were often difficult to identify as Chinese, both because of their names — Alberta, Criterion, BC, Grand Pacific, Victoria, Royal, or New York Café — and because they served Western as well as Chinese food.[1]

The first Cantonese restaurant in Montreal was started by a Chinese man, Hung Fung, in 1900,[2] and the first Chinese restaurant in Toronto was opened the following year by another, Sing Tom, under the name Sing Wing Restaurant, later changed to Kong Yu Teas.[3] We learn that "many of the restaurants did not serve Chinese dishes because they did not have the necessary ingredients or skilled cooks, and simply offered Western food — stews, chops, potatoes, vegetables, pies, stewed fruit and Jell-O."[4] They would prepare Chinese dishes by request only for their Chinese customers.

That eventually changed. As Chinatowns expanded in larger cities, the "restaurants offered Chinese cuisine, sometimes in modest upstairs rooms on oilcloth-covered tables, sometimes in sumptuous quarters with red, black and gold décor."[5] Chop suey houses didn't appear in the *Henderson Dictionary* of Edmonton until the mid-1920s, the first clear indication that Chinese food was available on regular menus.

There were strong Chinese Christian communities in many cities — Montreal, Winnipeg, Hamilton, and Toronto — and Chinese customs and food traditions became firmly established in many Canadian families. Picnics, garden parties, church suppers, and afternoon teas provided important cross-cultural influences.

In the 1920s, for instance, a confection called Chinese Chews appeared on the tea tables of the nation, along with Empire Cookies, Petit Fours, Melting Moments, and Pecan Snowballs. The main ingredients in Chinese Chews were walnuts, dates, and candied ginger, all linked in Canadian minds to the exotic Orient. The presence of China-trained Chinese missionaries and strong support from the United and Presbyterian churches contributed to the emergence from those communities of Chinese-Canadian leaders who understood how to bridge the gap between the ancient culture of Cathay and twentieth-century Canada, as indicated by Jean R. Burnet in her article in the book *Consuming Passions*: "When the children of Western missionaries returned to Canada they often retained their liking for Chinese food and introduced their friends to Chinese restaurants which were especially popular with impecunious students and others who enjoyed nutritious meals for low prices."[6]

We are fortunate to have an account of a Chinese restaurant in the early twentieth century in Brockville, Ontario, in the words of the owner's daughter, Valerie Mah:

> My parents were married on December 28, 1929. Six months later they opened a restaurant and called it the New York Café. Since Brockville is across the river from New York State, it was thought that the name might attract patrons. It was not a typical Chinese restaurant for that time because it had seating for almost 100, linen table cloths and napkins, and seafood from the East Coast. My father and his relatives opened

restaurants of the same name in Gananoque and Prescott, Ontario.

Weekly Chinese groceries came by trucks which stopped in the small communities between Toronto and Montreal. In our restaurant we served lobster from Conley in New Brunswick; fifty pounds were shipped by train in square boxes which had to be re-iced in Montreal. We picked up Winnipeg Goldeye and oysters in the market in Ottawa or Montreal or crossed the river by ferry to buy seafood shipped from New York. Our sturgeon came from the St. Lawrence River and sturgeon eggs were bottled and shipped to New York as caviar.[7]

Chinese families love to socialize and entertain. As restaurants opened in more Canadian communities, they could be found entertaining there instead of at home. Yum Cha or "drink tea" provided the opportunity to socialize, meet friends, and have fun. *Siu yeh*, "a little bit of food," could be a bedtime snack eaten in a restaurant. Eating *dim sum*, "touch the heart," those tiny mouth-watering steamed morsels, provided another social occasion. Those of us who aren't of Chinese ancestry learned to observe carefully those restaurants patronized by

Chinese Canadians and follow suit so we, too, could enjoy excellent Chinese cuisine.

Canadians of Chinese ancestry still celebrate many of the customs of their homeland. However, the biggest and most important is the Lunar New Year festival. This fifteen-day celebration marks the end of winter when new plants begin to appear in gardens and leaves will soon open on trees. It is a time of new beginnings and commences on the day of the first new moon after the sun enters Aquarius, between January 21 and February 20. Valerie Mah shares her description of this festival:

> New Year is one of the most important of three financial settling days and everyone desires to start the year with a clean slate. Debts are settled even if it means borrowing to pay off old debts and money is set aside for celebration.
>
> The Kitchen God presides over the kitchen and a week before New Year, on the 24th day of the 12th moon of the lunar calendar, he goes back to heaven to render a report to the Jade Emperor, believed to be responsible for rewards and punishments. Since people want to be on the Kitchen God's good side and hope he will hide their bad

deeds when he makes his report, they clean his shrine over the stove and offer him cakes and candies. Paper money can be burned to help with his travelling expenses or a paper horse burned for him to ride on. If this bribery is not enough, some smear his lips with molasses or sticky sweets or try to get him drunk by dipping his portrait in wine.

On New Year's Eve, the 30th day of the 12th moon, family members gather. Even the busiest of businesspeople plan to be home on New Year's Eve. It is a tradition on New Year's Eve to remember ancestors.

On New Year's Day, children and single adults greet parents and married relatives with *gung hei fat choi (gong xie fa chai)*, which means "may you have good fortune and riches," and the parents give them little red envelopes containing gifts of money. Red couplets, symbolizing virtue and sincerity, can be seen on either side of doorways of homes or in the community. These are always red, the sign of happiness and joy. Traditionally, families believe they can drive away evil spirits and bring good luck and prosperity at the same time.[8]

In Canadian cities where Chinese-Canadian families live, the lion and dragon dances have become part of New Year celebrations. Merchants hang out red envelopes with *li shi* or "lucky money," along with some green vegetables to "feed the lion." It is considered good luck for your establishment if the lion comes to your door. Two people operate the lion: one under its colourful and decorative head, the other beneath its equally colourful body. The money collected is given to community charities.

It is much more challenging to operate a dragon. The dragon creates much excitement, dispelling gloom, driving off evil spirits, spreading good fortune, and radiating the happy spirit of the New Year. The body is attached to poles that are waved back and forth by the sixteen occupants of the dragon to make it twist and turn.

The food at New Year's banquets is flavourful, colourful, and symbolic. Tangerines and oranges depict ingots of gold and represent happiness. Fish served whole is a sign of plenty, and if the fish's head points at you, it is considered very lucky. Vivid green vegetables represent jade, and peaches are a sign of immortality or long life. A vegetarian dish, *jhi*, is always served and includes *fat choy (fa cai)*, which means "prosperity," so everyone tries to have some of it. Lotus seeds are a sign of fertility and an abundance of sons.

The Lantern Festival, the fifteenth day of the first moon, signals the end of the New Year gala holiday. Many Chinese believe that spirits from heaven can be seen flying in the light of the first moon of the year and that seeing these spirits means good luck for the rest of one's life if one helped the spirits on their way. In former times lanterns lit the way of wandering souls to judgment and reincarnation, so a Ming emperor ordered ten thousand lamps to be set afloat on a lake. The sight was said to be so beautiful that Buddha descended from heaven to see it. Since the winter moon is always rather dim, torches are lit to throw artificial light on the elusive spirits. This festival helps to brighten the winter season and is the most popular and colourful of the entire welcome to the New Year.

We may not be experts at preparing Chinese dishes for our pleasure, but we can make these simple Chinese Chews that appeared in countless Canadian cookery books a century ago. Our ancestors were making and serving them, firm in the knowledge that they were preparing an exotic dainty to serve their families or guests.

CHINESE CHEWS

1 cup chopped walnuts
1 cup finely chopped dates
2 tablespoons chopped candied ginger
1 cup granulated sugar
¾ cup all-purpose flour
1 teaspoon baking powder

¼ teaspoon salt
2 eggs beaten
2 tablespoons melted butter

Combine walnuts, dates, ginger, and sugar in bowl. Combine flour, baking powder, and salt and add to first mixture. Blend in eggs and butter. Spread mixture in greased 8-inch-square pan and bake at 325 degrees for 25 minutes. While still warm, cut into small squares and shape each into a ball. Roll in sugar. Keep cool. Makes about three dozen.[9]

Happy New Year!

8

Shrove Tuesday:
The Feast Before the Fast

*He who wants Lent to seem short should contract
a debt to be repaid at Easter.*

— Italian Proverb

hrove Tuesday is a movable feast that occurs between February 2 and March 8. It is known to many Canadians as Pancake Day and is followed by Ash Wednesday, the beginning of Lent.

For centuries many Christians around the world have fasted for forty days prior to Easter Sunday when Jesus Christ rose from the dead. During Lent, as this period became known, Christians commemorated the forty days that Jesus spent fasting in the desert before his betrayal and crucifixion as described in the Bible.

Lent was, and continues to be, a time of fasting from several foods, including meat, fish, eggs, milk, butter, and other dairy products. The first day of Lent is called Ash Wednesday, and to prepare for this religious period it was customary in the days leading up to Ash Wednesday to go to Confession to have past sins forgiven and to be shriven of them by being given a penance to perform, thus the term *Shrove Tuesday* emerged. Knowing how difficult the fast would be, people would have one last celebration before it began.

Newcomers arriving in early Canada brought memories of the feasting, celebrations, fairs, and carnivals that were often held in their homelands in the days and weeks leading up to Lent when such frivolous activities wouldn't be tolerated. In England this period was called Shrovetide, in Germany it was Fetter Dienstag, and in France it was Mardi Gras, meaning "Fat Tuesday." Parades with costumed marchers and rough-and-tumble games were all part of those early Shrove Tuesday celebrations. In fact, it is believed that the modern game of football may have grown out of an annual contest in many communities where two teams of young people representing summer versus winter played a running game with a round object, usually an inflated animal bladder.

We learn that, in St. Leonard's, Newfoundland,

The day before Ash Wednesday was reserved strictly for special dinners and family entertainment in anticipation of the fast and abstinence of the Lenten season. Dancing, card-playing, weddings and public social gatherings were prohibited during the forty days of Lent.

Vegetables were taken from the cellar the previous evening and shared with neighbours who may not have had enough of the varieties to last up to this time of the year.

The puddings were mixed and put in separate pudding bags ahead of time. The meat (rabbit, venison, fresh beef or seabirds) were selected and made ready.

Breakfast consisted of oatmeal porridge, hot buttered toast and tea. There would be no strenuous labours executed this particular day. Only the milking and attending to the needs of the livestock, stocking firewood and making enough splits to carry over until Thursday. There would be no axe used on Ash Wednesday.

Dinner would be a generous meal of meats with rich brown gravy, figgy duff, bread puddings, peas puddings, cabbage, potatoes, turnips, carrots and salt beef. Sauce was always made to be served with left-over raisin or boiled bread pudding.

When the table was set, the family sat and grace was recited. Before eating, a little ceremony was performed to ensure a bountiful harvest and good luck … a small wooden toggle with a small piece of pudding, salt meat and cube of bread attached was hung over the outside door facing…. Pancakes were always the supper dish with symbols thrown in as a type of fortune-telling: ring = husband or wife; straw = famous; match = boatbuilder; nail = carpenter; button = bachelor or old maid; medal = priest or nun; money = rich man or woman; linen = tailor or seamstress.[1]

The making of pancakes was a very practical custom and used up the eggs, milk, and fat that would be taboo during Lent. Food historians believe that the original recipe for pancakes was simply meal and water cooked on a hot, flat stone to satisfy the appetite of an unsuccessful hunter or fisherman, and that it may be the oldest dish in the world. From that modest beginning, now lost in time, we find that pancakes have not only been an important symbol in Christian countries around the world for centuries but have also become a regular part of our Canadian diet at many times of the year.

Our Canadian ancestors, whether First Nations or new-comers, have made pancakes from cornmeal, buckwheat, and every possible type of flour. They have been fried on greased griddles (called by the Scots "girdles"), on flat hoe blades, and on hot, flat stones just as the first ones were cooked to serve travellers, families, or whole communities.

Over the years pancakes became a mainstay in many homes, served for breakfast, lunch, or supper. Many house-wives added yeast to their pancakes, homemade from hops or potatoes, to make them lighter. They would mix the batter the night before in a special pancake pitcher covered with a cloth and kept in a cool place. By morning the batter would have risen and was ready to ladle onto the griddle. After Lent ended, butter, maple syrup, honey, or molasses would often accom-pany the pancakes to the table.

During Lent, every housewife, mother, and cook needed imagination to vary the menu. From British Columbia comes a recipe that was "an old Lenten delicacy often eaten on Mothering Sunday":

FIG OR FAG PIE

Make a short crust shell, bake for lemon pie,
but use following filling:

2 cups cooked figs

¼ cup currants
¾ cup sugar
½ teaspoon mixed spices
1 tablespoon grated orange rind
1 tablespoon molasses
2 egg whites

Cut figs into small pieces, add sugar, currants, molasses, spices, and orange rind. Beat egg whites until stiff, but not dry, and fold into mixture, blending well. Pour into baked shell. Bake in a moderate oven (375 degrees) 30 minutes.

When cold, top with 1 cup heavy cream whipped with 2 tablespoons confectioners' sugar and 1 teaspoon vanilla. Topping is optional, and pie may be made as individual tarts.[2]

Across Canada the celebration of Shrove Tuesday is still observed by many families, while in others it is centred in the places of worship and community centres where pancake suppers provide local families with good food and fellowship regardless of their religious beliefs. Pancake suppers have been employed as fundraisers and as informal contests among the diners to prove who can consume the most pancakes at one sitting.

On the following day, Ash Wednesday, some Canadians may give up certain foods or do without something important to them until Lent ends on Holy Saturday. Others may remember with pleasure the feast of pancakes and agree with Will R. Bird, who writes in *Off Trail in Nova Scotia:*

> Stevens Mountains in the beautiful Wentworth Valley was settled by pre-Loyalists. One farmer had over five hundred bushels of buckwheat in one crop, and all threshing was then done by the flail. Buckwheat pancakes were a staple article on the menu, and when served with maple syrup made a breakfast fit for a king.

9

St. David's Day

*And there is good fresh trout for supper. My mother used to put them on
a hot stone over the fire, wrapped in breadcrumbs, butter, parsley and
lemon rind, all bound about with the fresh green leaves of leeks.
If there is better food in heaven, I am in a hurry to be there ...*

— Richard Llewellyn

For Canadians of Welsh ancestry, St. David's Day, March
1, is celebrated with music, stories, and the well-remem-
bered foods of their homeland much as it has been in
Wales since 1120. Like many other saints, little is known of
David's early life except that he lived in the sixth century and
died on March 1, probably in 589 A.D. His mother, Non

(possibly just "a nun"), was the daughter of Lord Cynyr of Caer Coch and gave birth to David on a clifftop during a violent storm.

His father, a chieftain, was related to King Arthur of the Round Table, and David was sent to a monastery school for many years to study the Bible. History tells us that he was renowned as a teacher and preacher. Many legends surround David and his good works: his great success in healing the sick, helping the poor, befriending orphans, protecting the helpless, winning hundreds of souls to Christianity, building chapels, and restoring or founding new monasteries.

It was said that daffodils burst into bloom on March 1 in his honour. David is also linked to the famous legend describing the victory of the last British king, Cadwaladr, over the Saxon foes when the Welsh soldiers who didn't wear uniforms were advised to pull leeks from nearby fields and put them in their hats so they would recognize one another and prevent accidental deaths. After the Welsh victory, the leek became the national emblem of Wales and today shares that distinction with the daffodil.

What are leeks? The leek (*Allium porrum*) is the mild, sweet cousin of onions, garlic, chives, shallots, and asparagus, all members of the lily family. The leek has a long, proud history stretching back to the Romans, who probably introduced it to the British Isles and to the Welsh.

Pottage, the earliest known dish of meat, herbs, and vegetables, was thickened with a cereal grain and cooked with water in one pot and eaten with a spoon. By the Middle Ages, two pottages had emerged — one that just contained cereal to become the ancestor of porridge, the other consisting of meat and vegetables. Leeks, which grew more easily in the Welsh climate than onions, were used to flavour both and were raised for Lent, as this poem confirms:

> Now leeks are in season for pottage full good,
> and spareth the milchcow and purgeth the
>   blood:
> These having with peason, for pottage in Lent,
> thou sparest both oatmeal and bread to be
>   spent.
> The gentry ate them in white porray.*

> Take the white of the leeks, and seeth them in a pot, and press them up, and hack them small on a board. And bake good almond milk, and a little rice, and do all these together, and seeth and stir it well, and do thereto sugar or honey and dress it in.[1]

[*Porray stems from the Latin *porum* (leek), but perhaps because of its likeness to purée came to be applied to thick pottages of green stuff in general. They were eaten by rich and poor alike and were a great standby of peasant families.]

Leeks weren't just popular in pottages and *porrays*. We also find them being protected, along with cabbages, by Welsh laws that insisted they should be fenced in against wandering cattle.[2] The vegetable also appears in historic recipes for seafood such as Limpet Pie, Fishguard Cawl, Leeks and Cabbages, Leek Pastry, Anglesey Eggs, and many more. It is appropriate that not only is St. David the patron saint of Wales but also of vegetarians!

New arrivals to Canada from Wales brought memories of other well-loved recipes and dishes, and because the basic ingredients needed were available, they continued the tradition of making Welsh Cakes, Welsh Gingerbread, Bara Brith, Pickled Red Cabbage, Lent Pudding, Griddle Scones, and Barm Brack (also a traditional Scottish and Irish recipe).[3]

The number of people of Welsh ancestry who came to Canada swelled to more than fifty thousand in the first half of the twentieth century. They soon formed St. David's and Welsh societies that stretched from coast to coast. Wherever the community is large enough, St. David's Day is celebrated with storytelling, music, banquets, and festive meals that can include Cawl Cennin (leek broth or soup) or Potato and Leek Soup, Lamb Stew or Roast Lamb, Faggots (a ball of seasoned, chopped liver or chopped offal baked or fried), peas, root vegetables, cabbage, Welsh Cakes, Welsh Rarebit, and pudding with a custard sauce.

The Dewi Sant Welsh United Church in Toronto was founded in 1907 by a group of like-minded Welsh immigrants who wanted to pray and socialize together. It was originally located on Clinton Street and in 1960 moved to its present site at 33 Melrose Avenue in Toronto. Sadly, it is the only Welsh church in Canada that gives its congregation the opportunity to keep in contact with their language and rich culture.[4]

The United Church Women have always been involved in fundraising by holding bake sales, bazaars, and strawberry teas. The Welsh are hospitable people, and from this "kitchen community" sprang the need to produce a book of homemade recipes, many brought from the homeland. Here is one that survived the voyage:

BARA BRITH

1 cup hot strong tea
1 cup raisins
¼ cup currants
1 cup brown sugar
1 beaten egg
2 cups flour
1 teaspoon baking powder
¼ teaspoon baking soda
¼ teaspoon salt

Soak overnight the first 3 ingredients. In the morning add brown sugar and beaten egg (no fats). Add remaining ingredients, mix well, and bake in a greased pan for 1½ hours in a 300-degree oven.[5]

The Dictionary of Gastronomy tells us that Bara Brith is a traditional Welsh cake, which literally translated means "speckled bread." There are two kinds of Bara Brith, both being popular — the rich fruit cake variety, eaten at Christmas time, and the bread or bun variety made with yeast and consumed with butter.[6]

Welsh Cakes are a national dish and are delicious when served with butter, honey, or jam. They are small, round cakes that can be made on a bakestone or girdle (griddle). The cakes are firm on the outside and soft within. The late Dorothy Grove of Toronto brought her favourite Welsh Cake recipe with her when she left Wales for Canada in the twentieth century:

WELSH CAKES

2 cups flour
1 teaspoon baking powder
½ cup sugar
⅔ cup lard
1 egg
½ cup currants

½ teaspoon salt
½ teaspoon allspice, nutmeg, or mace
1 teaspoon vanilla

Mix all ingredients well, roll out about ¼ inch thick, cut into circles, and cook over medium heat in a greased cast-iron frying pan until brown on both sides.[7]

10

Sap's Running!

The rising of the sap is felt in the forest trees; frosty nights and sunny days call forth the activity of the settlers in the woods; sugar making is now at hand, and all is bustle and life in the shanty.

— Catharine Parr Traill, *The Canadian Settlers' Guide*

With the words of this chapter's title, one of Canada's oldest industries prepares to swing into action and thousands of winter-weary Canadians get ready to celebrate the coming of spring. Over the centuries the annual tapping of maple, butternut, and black walnut trees has brought a joyful end to winter while providing a sweetener, a flavouring, and an opportunity to enjoy good food, fun, and fellowship.

Long before European contact, the First Nations watched for the "sugar moon" to appear, for that was the signal that the magic sap was running and they should gather in camps near groves of trees to begin the harvest. This gift proved that the Creator was again providing for their needs, and they would celebrate with feasting, thanksgiving, and the telling of the stories and legends the involved the harvest. The Iroquois Nation has a legend that tells of Hiawatha's grandmother, Nokomis, who showed a tribal hero, Manabusha, how to tap trees. The sap came from the trees in a thick syrup, and Manabusha was concerned that his people wouldn't appreciate something that was so easy. He climbed to the top of the tallest maple tree and poured water over it to dilute the sap. Then he instructed his people to chop wood, build a bonfire, fashion bark containers, and stir the sap while it thickened into syrup, thus ensuring they would appreciate and treasure the harvest.

The First Nations employed a simple method of tapping trees by making a diagonal incision in the trunk and inserting a strip of bark at the lower end of the cut to serve as a spile. The sap dripped into birchbark containers placed beside the trees. When the containers were full, the sap was poured into hollowed-out logs. Hot rocks were placed in the sap over and over again to heat it and evaporate the excess liquid. This long, slow process eventually resulted in the sap becoming syrup and finally sugar.

Sap's Running!

The Natives began their festival of thanksgiving by passing around ceremonial containers of syrup so that everyone could sample it and be strengthened by this energy-building medicine. They feasted on foods flavoured with syrup, such as soups, puddings, fish, fowl, and game. Quantities of the thick syrup were poured into cooling troughs and kneaded until it was thick and creamy. This soft sugar was then transferred into moulds and stored to be eaten as a sweet, used as a flavouring and preservative during the coming year, or as a barter item with other nations.

The sugar maple tree grows mainly in eastern Canada — Quebec, Ontario, Nova Scotia, and New Brunswick — as well as in the northeastern United States from Minnesota to Maine and south to West Virginia. Sugar maples are now rare west of the Ontario border. However, Jonathan Carver describes a very different situation in 1796 when he came upon Lake Winnipeg (Manitoba):

> Lake Winnpeck, or as the French write it, Lac Ouinipoque, has in the north-east some mountains, and on the east many barren plains. The maple or sugar tree grows here in great plenty, and there is likewise gathered an amazing quantity of rice, which proves that grain will flourish in these northern climates as well as in warmer.[1]

The colonists from the Old World were delighted to find this unexpected and inexpensive source of flavouring and sugar that appeared each spring. They quickly learned the simple skills of tapping the trees and transforming the sap into syrup and sugar. Elizabeth Simcoe, the wife of John Graves Simcoe, the first lieutenant governor of Upper Canada, describes in her *Diary* the simple process of extracting sap from trees:

Wednesday, March 19, 1794

This is the night for making maple sugar; a hot sun and frosty nights cause the sap to flow most. Slits are cut in the bark of the trees, and wooden troughs set under the tree, into which the sap — a clear, sweet water — runs. It is collected from a number of trees and boiled in large kettles till it becomes a hard consistence. Moderate boiling will make powder sugar, but when boiled long it forms very hard cakes, which are better.... In a month's time when the sap is exhausted, an inferior kind runs, of which vinegar is made. Cutting the trees does not kill them, for the trees bear it for

many years following. Dr. Nooth at Quebec,
showed me some maple sugar which he has
refined, and it became as white as West
India sugar.[2]

Joseph Bouchette, surveyor general of Lower Canada
(Quebec), was widely travelled and describes the sugar-mak-
ing operation in that province in 1796:

In the spring, when the sap begins to rise in
the (maple) trees, the habitants repair to the
woods, furnished with kettles, troughs, and
all the necessary apparatus for carrying on
the manufacture, where they form a tem-
porary encampment; the mode of collect-
ing the sap is by making an incision in the
tree, into which is inserted a thin bit of stick
to serve as a conductor from whence, an
hour or two after sunrise, the sap begins to
trickle down into a trough placed to receive
it; when a sufficient quantity of this liquor
is obtained from several trees, it is put into
an iron kettle and boiled, until it comes to
the consistence of a thick syrup; it is then
cooled, and afterwards subjected to another
process of boiling and clarifying. When this

is sufficiently performed in proportion to the degrees of purity they intend to give it, it is put into vessels of different sizes to harden, containing from half a pound to eight or ten pounds. Its colour is of all shades between a dark and light brown, according to the care that is taken in clarifying it; indeed, by a repetition of the process it may be rendered as white as common refined sugar. Being considered very wholesome, the use of it is general among the country people for all purposes, and the consumption of it is considerable in families of respectability for ordinary occasions; the price of it varies from three pence halfpenny to six-pence per pound. It is consistently to be had in the market of Quebec.[3]

From Estelle (Desjardins) Fleury, we have a very detailed, personal report of her Métis family's harvest of this precious resource over three generations:

The making of maple syrup and maple sugar has a history as old as the province itself. In the early days maple sugar was the only sweetening available. Grandfather Alexander

Allard tapped maple trees for this purpose. He made an axe slash in the tree and inserted a chip or a thin piece of peeled red willow to convey the sap to a pail below.

A large 45 gallon cast iron kettle was used. Old dry wood was gathered beforehand. Empty 40 gallons of sap into the kettle; make a fire under the pot and boil the sap for 8 hours adding more dry wood when needed. Then let the fire burn down. Stop one hour to cool. Using a soup ladle, carefully put the maple syrup into another container, making sure to leave one quart of syrup in the bottom of the kettle. Slowly pour in some water and then add more sap for another batch of syrup. This is to prevent cracking the hot kettle. After approximately 7 to 8 hours of boiling, there will be 1 gallon of thick syrup. Further boiling of the syrup in the house on the stove (carefully so as not to burn it) will produce 12 small muffin tins of maple sugar.[4]

The sap flows in the sapwood of the tree from mid-March to late April. Nights with temperatures below the freezing point must be followed by warm, sunny days with thawing temperatures (up to eight degrees Celsius) to make the sap flow. The fickle Canadian weather could catch a new farmer off guard with a sudden change in the weather. John Lynch recommends in his report on Grey County (Ontario) how to be prepared:

> As you will not have much other work the first winter, you should not only chop what will be required for your spring crop, but something towards your summer fallow for fall wheat. If you have a good "sugar-bush" you should prepare a sufficient number of sap-troughs, of pine timber, if you can get it; but failing that, black ash is the next best.[5]

A sugar bush was an important asset to a pioneer farmer, and the quantity of sugar that could be produced from a fifty-acre farm shouldn't be underestimated. This description by W. Clemens, a new immigrant from Wiltshire, England, who settled in Port Talbot, Upper Canada, in October 1830, gives a fair estimate of the harvest:

> I like the country very much. I am at liberty to shoot turkeys, quail, pigeon, and all kinds of game which I have in my back wood. I have also a sugar bush which will

make me a ton of sugar yearly. The timber is very fine. We sow but one bushel of wheat to an acre, and the increase is about 50. The land in general is black peat and sandy loam. My wife and two sons are all well and happy, and thankful that they have arrived over safe. Cows are worth from 50s. Sheep, large and fat, are worth 10s. 6d. No poor-rate, no taxes, no overseer, no beggars. The wheat that is left in the field would keep a whole parish.[6]

It wasn't until 1854 that John Redpath, a leading Montreal businessman, built the first sugar refinery in Canada known as the Canada Sugar Refinery, so maple syrup and maple sugar continued to fulfill a specific need in the Canadian diet as a sweetener in the nineteenth century. As well as serving a family's needs and being used as a barter item among neighbours, maple sugar was a very saleable product at the local farmers' market, as Andrew Oliver describes in his guidebook to intended immigrants:

Canadian sugar, which is drawn from maple trees, is brought to the market in cakes, and sold at 5d and 6d the pound. Tobacco sold in the leaf, but twisted like ropes of straw,

and coiled up, may be purchased very low.
I saw a coil, weighing eight pounds, for 6s;
but that which is manufactured in Britain is
preferable.[7]

Imported flavourings were always scarce and expensive in the pioneer communities in Canada, so the subtle and unique flavour that resulted from adding maple to a recipe was highly regarded. As a result, recipes for maple tarts, maple sugar biscuits, maple beer, maple butter, and maple cream began to appear in handwritten manuscript books and printed cookbooks. Traditional recipes for muffins, pies, cookies, cakes, cake frosting, rice pudding, and Indian pudding were all improved by substituting maple syrup or maple sugar for the usual flavourings and sweeteners. Unusual recipes featuring maple products appeared, including Backwoods Pie, Wit's End Pudding, Crow's Nest, Maple Apples, and the favourite Maple Sugar Candy.

It wasn't long before the newcomers realized that the production of maple syrup and sugar was an intriguing, romantic operation. Recalling First Nations celebrations, French Canadians soon organized their own festivals for sugaring-off at the sugar shanties or shacks in the bush. Originally, a Festival de la Cabane à Sucre would have included only close family and friends and would have been a very personal celebration.

Sap's Running!

Micheline Mongrain-Dontigny, author of *Traditional Quebec Cooking: A Treasure of Heirloom Recipes*, gives us a description that still prevails of a traditional sugar party:

> As soon as the sugar maker has enough maple products to feed many people, sugar parties are organized for family and friends. Everybody meets at the sap house where the maple sap is taken to be boiled down from which all of the delicious maple products are obtained. Many give a helping hand to gather the maple sap and everyone shares a meal of dishes which have been prepared with plenty of maple syrup poured on top. The best part of the meal is the dessert which consists of hot maple taffy poured onto fresh snow. Guests are invited to go outside, where they are given a spatula to roll the taffy while it is still warm.
>
> After the meal, tables are put aside and the party goes on with singing and dancing until the end of the evening.[8]

If there were children present, they would pounce on the taffy as it hardened in the snow. From this simple beginning, "taffy pulls" became a popular event with younger folk. If maple syrup wasn't available, molasses, sugar, and butter were boiled, poured onto a well-buttered platter until cool enough to handle, and then pulled until it became firm and turned golden.

The sugar party soon became the sugar social, and the foundation was laid for a profitable business. The season was short but merry, and memories like those of E.A. Howes, a small boy turned schoolteacher in Glengarry County in eastern Ontario in the 1880s, are shared in his book *With a Glance Backward*:

> The house would be crowded but "the more the merrier." Milk pans, dish pans, pans of all description, as long as they were big enough, were packed with snow. A large boiler filled with syrup or broken sugar was placed on the stove and carefully tended. When the contents of the boiler had reached the required consistency, which could be decided after repeated tastings, quantities were ladled out upon the snow, where it congealed into the finest confection man has ever encountered here below. The paying guests were armed with a table fork and given the personal responsibility that they secured the worth of their money. There was nothing particularly refined about the whole affair but there was a

happy lack of constraint; since no authority had ever dared to lay down rules of etiquette for such a function there were no rules to be broken. The only restriction was individual capacity, and this was a matter of only private concern; each was master of his own fate and did not worry about it. The Sugar Social was always popular and profitable ...[9]

11

St. Patrick's Day

May the Irish hills caress you.
May her lakes and rivers bless you.
May the luck of the Irish enfold you.
May the blessings of St. Patrick behold you.

—Irish Blessing

The early years of St. Patrick, who became the patron saint of Ireland, are shrouded in mystery. It is believed by some historians that he was born in Scotland, while others think it was England or Wales. Legend tells us that the boy, Maewyn, was captured by pirates at age sixteen and sold into slavery to an Irish chieftain. He escaped, travelled to France, studied for the priesthood, and in 432 A.D. Pope Celestine made him a bishop.

Patrick returned to Ireland with the difficult mission of converting the many Irish tribes to Christianity and belief in one god. Legend also says that Patrick explained the Trinity (Father, Son, and Holy Ghost united as one) by showing the three-leafed shamrock to the people as an example of three separate units joined to form one whole. St. Patrick must have been aware of the fact that the shamrock was the sacred plant of the Druids of Ireland, because its leaves formed a triad: a group of three, three being a mystical number to the Druids, as in many religions.

The legend of the shamrock is connected with that of the banishment of serpents from Ireland by the conviction that snakes are never seen on a trefoil — a leaf of three parts. Tradition also states that such plants are a remedy against the stings of snakes and scorpions.

As time passed, the reverence and legends surrounding St. Patrick became the folklore of everyday life. When he died on March 17, probably in 493 A.D., he had accomplished his dream of Ireland becoming one country under God. St. Patrick's Day on March 17 was declared a holy day and a public holiday. It was celebrated with religious ceremonies and the wearing of shamrocks, green ribbons, and other items of green apparel.

The day was set aside from the Lenten fast, and traditional foods and special dishes graced tables, with potatoes the centrepiece of the meal. Cooks celebrated the day by adding raisins and currants to Lenten bread and marking their loaves with the sign of the cross before baking. Wherever they travelled as merchants, soldiers, sailors, and servants, the Irish carried the memory of this day and how it was celebrated in their hearts and minds "at home."

New arrivals in Canada of Irish ancestry swelled the population of many communities, including Halifax, where by 1760 the Irish constituted a third of the population. They included disbanded soldiers and sailors, indentured servants, and some pretending to be English to circumvent the law banning Irish Catholics from the province.

The Charitable Irish Society, founded in Halifax in 1786, promoted Irish involvement in the welfare of the community, and ten years later at a St. Patrick's Day feast the guests included His Royal Highness, Prince Edward, Sir John Wentworth (the colonial administrator for Nova Scotia), some members of Council, the Speaker, and several members of the House![1]

It is believed that the potato, the vegetable the Irish loved so well, was introduced to Europe by Sir Walter Raleigh on a return voyage from the New World. They grew in popularity until it was said the typical Irish peasant family ate about eight pounds of potatoes daily. No wonder then that the country was devastated in 1845 and the years following as crop after crop failed, leaving a million people dead and another million destitute. A mass migration began from Ireland to British

North America, Australia, and New Zealand. Sharon Doyle Driedger in *An Irish Heart* details the Great Famine and traces many of these new arrivals to Montreal and the community they created — "Griffithtown: the Irish Capital of Canada." Toronto also had an Irish community called Cabbagetown, because the new arrivals loved cabbage and used every available inch of space around their homes to grow the vegetable for their own tables and for sale.

There were many newcomers of Irish ancestry already settled in Canada. However, thousands can trace the arrival of their families to those hungry years. They brought with them not only their traditions and memories of this holy day and national holiday honouring St. Patrick but also their love of traditional foods, with the potato being the most desirable ingredient to have in their larders.

From Lieutenant Governor Archibald on the occasion of the centennial celebrations in Stewiacke, Nova Scotia, in 1880, we have a glimpse of an Irish settler's meal in Nova Scotia:

> As to the outfit for meals, not much was required. A tin teapot, delft cups and saucers, wooden handled knives and two pronged steel forks. Two large soup plates, one for meat, the other for potatoes, were all the dishes required for the table. The meat was either pork or beef. Before cooking it was

cut into morsels called bites and put into a pan with fat and fried over the fire — when cooked, it was poured into one of the plates mentioned, which, with the potatoes in the other plate, were placed in the middle of the bare deal table. The family drew around, each one helped himself to a potato, peeled it, cut it into morsels, and then with his fork selected a bite out of the meat plate according to his fancy. Sometimes he dipped a slice of potato into the melted fat in the dish and withdrew it saturated with the luscious fluid.

When there were young children, two or three of them could be accommodated around the frying pan on the hearth. The mother had taken care to leave some of the fat and a few "bites" of meat in the pan, and had sliced some potatoes into it, stirring the whole together, and the children arranging themselves around the pan, helped themselves with spoons.[2]

At first the three daily meals were very much the same, with bread, potatoes, pork, or beef as the mainstays. As soon as mills were built, oats were used for porridge and oatcakes and as an ingredient in other recipes.

After Irish families became established and developed farms, they harvested potatoes from their fields and gardens and stored them in barrels of sand or sawdust for the winter months. They were boiled, fried, creamed, and scalloped and utilized to make yeast, soup, bread, scones, salads, pies, Irish stew, and stuffing (particularly for wild geese). Potato flour was made of cooked, dried, and ground potatoes and was employed to thicken soups, sauces, gravies, and puddings. When St. Patrick's Day arrived, there were many dishes for the feast that were always accompanied by music.

From Newfoundland we have glimpses of the pleasure of celebrating St. Patrick's Day:

> The day was set apart from Lenten fast so that an Irish concert could be put on in the parish hall at night. The concert was followed by a dance and the music of fiddle, accordion, tin whistle or mouth organ could be heard until the stroke of twelve. Then it was back to fasting for the rest of Lent.[3]

> There were times of much merriment on Pancake Night, the eve of Lent and the feast of St. Patrick. Old time dances, the music of the fiddle or the accordion gives the gay throng the necessary accompaniment. One

> glad interlude is the singing of some folk
> songs by some virtuoso or the dancing of a
> hornpipe by a professional heel and toe artist.[4]

The diners, dancers, singers, and musicians had partaken of Newfoundland favourites, including Potato Cakes, Irish Soda Bread, Boxty (flour, butter, salt, pepper), Calcannon (also called Call Cannon or Kohl Cannon), with combinations of potatoes, carrots, turnips, cabbages, leeks, milk, butter, salt, and pepper.

On St. Patrick's Day, Canadians of Irish ancestry, and those who wish they were, will prepare or find their personal feast in remembrance of St. Patrick. Here are some simple suggestions:

> For your St. Patrick's Day centerpiece: A
> white geranium with clover seeds pushed in
> the soil around it. Plan ahead as the seeds
> will take about three weeks to germinate!
> Begin with a small bare tree branch
> and anchor it firmly in a base. Trim the tree
> with paper shamrocks, bank the base with
> potatoes. For place cards use toy clay pipes;
> names penciled on the stems, Serve lime
> sherbet and shamrock-shaped cookies.[5]

You may also want to add salad to the menu:

St. Patrick's Day

SHAMROCK SALAD

Wash green pepper. Cut thin slice from stem end; remove seeds and tongue. Pack with cheese mixed with salad dressing. Chill; slice with sharp knife. Pimentos, nuts and olives could be added. Serve on lettuce, watercress or endives.[6]

Afternoon tea has been, and continues to be, a popular way to entertain. Here is another suggestion that our ancestors might have used:

TEA WITH A TOUCH OF IRELAND

Long Slices of Buttered Irish Soda Bread
Pot of Hot Tea

The Irish were also famous for their fruit-cake; so if you wish, substitute it.[7]

Soda bread was, and is, to the Irish what bannock means to the Scots, and was at first cooked on a girdle (later called a griddle). It could also be baked in a Dutch oven, since this utensil was popular for those without an oven. The Dutch oven is a large iron pot with a tight-fitting lid that can be set near the coals in a fireplace, with the lid put in place and coals piled on until the bread, pie, or cake is baked.

Still a favourite on our tables across Canada is Irish Soda Bread. Often it is the historic "sample" offered to visitors in historic house museums who interpret the life and times of Irish settlers. Here is a popular recipe that appears in many of our ancestors' cookery books:

IRISH SODA BREAD

4 cups all-purpose flour
¼ cup sugar
1 teaspoon salt
1 teaspoon baking powder
¼ cup butter
2 cups seedless raisins
1⅓ cup buttermilk
1 egg
1 teaspoon baking soda

Mix flour, sugar, salt, and baking powder. Cut in butter with two knives until it resembles coarse meal. Stir in raisins. Combine buttermilk, egg, and baking soda. Stir into flour mixture until just moistened. Bake in greased one quart pudding pan or casserole at 375 degrees for 45 to 50 minutes or until it is golden brown.

Remember, flour a knife and make lengthwise and crosswise mark in the dough in the form of a cross before putting it in the oven.[8]

May the luck of the Irish be with you! Or as an Irish blessing says: "May St. Patrick guard you wherever you go, and guide you in whatever you do, and may his loving protection be a blessing to you always."

The above blessing was, and is, often given on special occasions or at festive meals when the Irish gather to celebrate. If you would like to travel back in time and savour a menu for just such a meal that your ancestors might have enjoyed in Canada a century ago, the one on the next page has been carefully preserved between the pages of a family Bible and only recently discovered by family members. The testimonial that is handwritten on the printed menu is a fine endorsement: "We were at this dinner & it was good."[9]

We were at this dinner & it was good.

OIRISH DINNER

Here's to the harp of Tara's halls,
Here's to the shamrock that grows
'neath her walls;
Here's to St. Patrick's Day,
Re-tune your harps and play.
Here's to the Emerald Isle;
Keep up Old Erin's style.

THURSDAY, MARCH SIVINTEENTH
From 5.30 to 8 p.m.

Killarney Soup 10c   Oirish Shtew 20c

Rashers uf the Baste and White Wings 25c

Illegent Shteak Poi 10c.

Phork and Banes, Bridget Shtoile 15c

Mashed Praties 10c   Colleen Bawn Paze 10c

Murphies in their Jackets 5c

Grane Apple Poi, Oirish Stoile 10c   Pumpkin Poi 10c

Coffay 5c   Tay 5c   Butthermilk 5c

BHOYS, RALLY 'ROUND THE SHAMROCK

UNDER THE AUSPICES OF THE METHODIST LADIES' AID

12

Celebrations of Survival:
Purim and Passover

Let all who are hungry come and eat. Let all who are in need
come and celebrate the Passover with us.

As Britain and France struggled for possession of the
northern regions of North America, it was the French
who established the first permanent settlements.
During the first one hundred and fifty years of the French
regime, immigration was low, averaging only sixty-six persons
a year. It is sometimes considered to have been confined, as
the official policy long required, to French Roman Catholics.
However, there is the well-documented case of Esther Brandeau,
a young Jewish woman who went to New France disguised as a
boy in 1738 and spent a year there.

The British were more receptive, and John Frankes of Jewish ancestry was granted the first settlement grant in British North America in the Halifax allotment soon after it was founded in 1749.[1] Slowly, Jewish communities began to develop in Montreal, Quebec City, Trois-Rivières, and other communities.[2]

When newcomers of Jewish ancestry arrived in Canada, they, like all the other newcomers, brought with them their beliefs, religion, folklore, and food traditions. They also conveyed their calendar, which is both solar and lunar. The years are reckoned by the sun and the months by the moon. Each month begins with the appearance of a new moon, and because the calendar starts with creation, the number of years recorded doesn't correspond with the Western reckoning of B.C and A.D.[3] Like many other calendars, it commences with the basic unit of the day from sundown to sundown.

Jewish Canadians celebrate many holidays throughout the year, as well as one every week — the Sabbath or Shabbat, which falls on Saturday and is a day of rest. It begins at sundown on Friday evening and is based on traditions that are similar to those that have been observed for thousands of years. History tells us that a *shofar* made from a ram's horn was blown at sundown to summon the ancient Hebrews home from their work in the fields. They bathed, put on clean clothes, and ate a special Sabbath dinner that included *challah*, a fine white bread made from sifted white flour, honey, and eggs.

Over time, candlesticks and wine became part of the celebration. Blessings continued to be said or sung, and the bread was divided among everyone present. Today, on Saturday mornings, Jewish people attend prayers at synagogues and exchange the greeting *Shabbat shalom*, or "peaceful Sabbath."

Two holidays that fall in the spring are celebrations of survival — Purim and Passover. Purim, celebrated in February or March, is the most festive of all Jewish holidays and includes costumes, prizes, noisemakers, and of course special foods.

The story of Purim is told in the Book of Esther in the Tanakh, the Hebrew Old Testament. Esther was a beautiful young Jewish woman, the queen of King Ahasuerus of Persia when Haman, one of the king's advisers, was plotting to destroy the Jewish people. Haman was casting lots, known as *purim*, to decide what day he would carry out his evil plot. When Esther learned of the scheme, she fasted for three days, then approached the king and told him of her people's fate. The king sentenced Haman to death, and the Jewish people have rejoiced over the centuries on the fourteenth and fifteenth days of Adar, the twelfth month of their calendar.

This is a time first of fasting in memory of Esther's three-day fast, followed by feasting with Hamantaschen, a three-cornered cookie with a pocket filled with apricot or prune jam or sweetened poppy seeds, named for Haman's three-cornered hat. Hamantaschen are accompanied by other festive dishes, and Purim is a joyous time and an occasion for members of the Jewish community to remember others and to send out small gifts of food or drink such as candy, fruit, or wine, and to make gifts to charity.[4]

BASIC HAMANTASCHEN DOUGH

4 eggs
1 cup sugar
1 cup oil
2 tablespoons homogenized honey
¼ teaspoon vanilla
dash of salt
3 cups flour (approximately)
1 teaspoon baking powder

Beat eggs and sugar well; add honey. Add oil slowly, then salt, vanilla, flour, and baking powder, until dough is workable. Divide into 4 portions. Roll into ¼-inch thickness on a floured board. Cut in 3-inch circles. Place a teaspoon of filling in the centre of each circle. Form triangles by folding three sides to the centre. Bake on greased baking sheet at 400 degrees for 12 to 15 minutes. Yield 4 to 5 dozen.

HAMANTASCHEN FILLING

Prune filling:

> 1 pound pitted prunes (soaked)
> 1 cup sultana light raisins
> 1 lemon
> ½ cup sugar
> 1 tablespoon honey

Soak prunes overnight or for 2 hours in hot water. Put prunes and raisins through food chopper; grate the whole lemon very fine. Mix all ingredients together.[5]

Passover, or Pesach, commemorates the freedom of Jewish slaves from Egypt during the reign of Pharaoh Ramses II. About three thousand years ago a Jewish shepherd called Moses was instructed by God to ask the pharaoh to free the Jewish people. When the pharaoh refused, God unleashed ten plagues, including the slaying of the first-born son in every family. God instructed Moses to have the slaves mark the doorposts of their homes with lambs' blood so they would be "passed over" or "protected" by the Angel of Death. The pharaoh finally relented and told the Jews to leave. However, they packed so hurriedly that they didn't have time to bake bread or even to leaven the dough and let it rise.

When the Jews reached the Red Sea, they realized that the pharaoh's army was in pursuit to bring them back. Miraculously, the water parted and allowed them to cross to freedom. When the soldiers attempted to follow, they were drowned.

Centuries later this miracle was, and is, celebrated for eight days with the first two and last two holidays. In preparation homes are cleansed of all yeast foods, or *hametz*, and special utensils and pots and pans are brought out and used to make and serve the special foods. No leavened foods are consumed for eight days.

Over the eve of Pesach, families often travelled long distances to gather for the traditional Seder. This is both a meal and worship service performed in order, as described in an ancient book called the Haggadah. As the meal is eaten, the symbolism of each of the traditional foods is explained. The Seder table is set with a special Seder plate that includes five traditional symbolic foods: a roasted lamb bone (sacrificial lamb); a green herb (parsley representing fruits of the earth); bitter herbs (horseradish, as it was bitter to be a slave); a mixture of chopped nuts, apples, and a wine called charoset (signifying the red clay used for bricks); and a roasted egg (regular offerings in the temple). Matzoh, or unleavened bread, is a combination of flour and water and is served as a reminder of the hurried flight to leave Egypt. Many families invite special guests to join them for the Passover Seder: "Let all who are hungry come and eat."

During the following days of celebration, beef brisket, chicken soup with matzoh balls, horseradish, hard-boiled eggs, roasted root vegetables, gefilte fish, potato pancakes, jam, chocolate macaroons, and honey cakes are all part of this joyous time of thanksgiving and celebration.

Many of the Jewish families who arrived in Manitoba in the late nineteenth and early twentieth centuries have shared their treasured family recipes in *Manitoba's Heritage Cookery*. One of the most popular is:

CHALAH

1 teaspoon sugar
½ cup warm water
1 package yeast
3 cups flour (approximately)
2–3 tablespoons sugar or honey
1 teaspoon salt
⅓ cup oil
2 eggs
¼ cup lukewarm water
1 egg yolk beaten with 1 teaspoon water
poppy or sesame seeds

Dissolve sugar in ½ cup warm water in measuring cup. Sprinkle yeast over and let stand for 8 to 10 minutes. Stir to dissolve. Place flour, sugar, and salt in large bowl. Pour dissolved yeast mixture over. Mix well. Add oil and eggs and continue to mix. Add water and continue to mix until dough begins to mass. Add flour if necessary. Dough should be sticky. Turn out onto a lightly floured board. Knead for 1 to 2 minutes, until smooth and elastic, adding just enough flour to prevent dough from sticking to your hands or to the board.

Round up in a large greased bowl, cover with a towel and let rise in a warm place until double in bulk. (Dough may also be placed in refrigerator to rise. It can be kept up to 3 days before shaping and baking.) Punch down. If you have time, let the dough rise once again, or you may shape it at this point.

Divide dough into 3 equal portions. Roll with you hands into 3 long strands. Place on a greased baking sheet. Braid and then tuck ends under. Cover with a towel and let rise until double. Brush with beaten egg yolk and sprinkle with seeds. Bake at 400 degrees in the lower third of the oven for 30 minutes, until golden brown and dough sounds hollow when tapped with your fingers. Cool away from drafts. Yield: 1 large loaf. Freezes well.[6]

When a dessert is to be served and leavening agents aren't allowed, an arrangement of fresh fruit and a small homemade chocolate treat or a few Meringue Kisses may be the perfect ending to a perfect meal:

MERINGUE KISSES

3 egg whites
¾ cup sugar

Beat egg whites in a bowl until very light, then gradually beat in sugar. Line a cookie sheet with parchment paper and carefully spoon a small amount onto it. This mixture should make about 45 to 50 kisses. Bake in preheated 300-degree oven for 25 to 30 minutes. Turn off oven and let kisses cool in the oven for a few hours. Remove when they are dry and firm.

13

God's Day

And when they came to the place, which is called Calvary,
there they crucified him, and the malefactors,
one on the right hand, and the other on the left.

— Luke 23:33

As Lent draws to a close, Good Friday (probably called
God's Day originally) commemorates the death of
Jesus Christ by crucifixion. Many cultural groups fast
on this day, while others feast as a symbol of the continua-
tion of life. There are solemn parades in many communities,
sometimes called the Way of the Cross, portraying Jesus's
life, betrayal, trial, and crucifixion. In Italian communities

thousands turn out to watch processions commemorating the Passion of Christ. These depict the final weeks of Jesus's life, including his trial and condemnation by Pontius Pilate and his crucifixion. For more than five decades this event has been held in Toronto and is considered the largest presentation in North America. Services of mourning are conducted in many Christian churches across Canada, and Hot Cross Buns have become a national symbol of this day.

Meat and wine were always forbidden on this day, and centuries ago Pope Gregory I (540–604 A.D.) directed that only bread, salt, and vegetables could be eaten. Bread scored with a cross was known in Egypt and Greece and was used by Saxon pagans long before Christianity emerged, but it was reinterpreted as the cross of Christ in England when the country was converted. Hot Cross Buns were marked with the sign of salvation, and as early as 1225 bakers in England had a thriving trade in Hot Cross Buns on Good Friday. They became a popular street food as they were peddled through the lanes and byways of towns with the jingle:

> Hot cross buns!
> Hot cross buns!
> One a penny, two a penny,
> Hot cross buns!
> If your daughters do not like them,
> Give them to your sons;

But if you haven't any of these pretty little elves
You cannot do better than eat them yourselves.[1]

English settlers brought folklore to Canada involving Hot Cross Buns, including the practice of placing a bun high on a chimney shelf, fireplace, or stove for every absent family member to bring him or her safely home. If two people shared a bun, they would know true fellowship. Legend also tells us that sailors wore them on cords around their necks to protect them from illness or shipwreck.

If you would like to make your own Hot Cross Buns, here is a simple recipe that appeared in the *Canadian Cook Book* in 1923 and has been enjoyed by countless Canadian families ever since:

HOT CROSS BUNS

1 cup milk
⅓ cup sugar
1 teaspoon salt
⅛ cup lukewarm water
1 package yeast
3 tablespoons soft butter
1 tablespoon cinnamon
½ cup dried fruit (raisins or currants)
about 3 cups flour

Make a sponge with warm milk, butter, sugar, and salt. Cool. Add yeast that has softened in warm water. Add flour sifted with cinnamon, and dried fruit. Knead until elastic. Let rise in warm place until light. Knead lightly again and shape into buns or large biscuits. Make cuts at right angles on the top of biscuit. Let rise, bake in moderate oven for 25 to 30 minutes. At end of 15 minutes, glaze by brushing buns with a mixture of 1 tablespoon sugar and 2 tablespoons milk.[2]

Today Hot Cross Buns aren't just baked and eaten on Good Friday. They are found in markets and bakeries for many months of the year, a testament to their popularity and perhaps to the faith Canadians have in their power to protect us year-long.

14

He Is Risen!

And He departed from our sight that we might return to our heart,
and there find Him. For He departed, and behold, He is here.

— St. Augustine

For Christians, not only in Canada but around the world, Easter is believed to be the greatest religious festival of the year. It was on this day centuries ago that Jesus Christ, who was crucified, died, and was buried on God's Day (Good Friday), rose from his grave, walked among his disciples, and urged his followers to go with him to Galilee.

The Resurrection on Easter Day, as it became known, is synonymous with a celebration stretching back centuries before Christianity and named for Eostre, the Anglo-Saxon goddess of spring. She was believed to have opened the gates of Valhalla so Baldur, the Sun God, could bring light to Earth. The festival named in her honour was called Eostur and was held at each vernal equinox on March 21.

Originally, the Christian churches celebrated Easter every Sunday as they expected their Lord's return. Eventually, in 325 A.D., during the reign of Constantine the Great, Easter was decreed to be on the first Sunday after the full moon at or immediately following the vernal equinox, which means it can fall between March 22 and April 25.

During those ancient celebrations of rejoicing at the spring sun's triumph over the cold death of winter, many foods were believed to have magical qualities and were encrusted with legends of fertility and good fortune. For example, the egg formed an enigma in itself and was looked upon as representing the origins of life. Aristophanes, the Greek comic dramatist, described the great bird that laid the world egg. According to Kalevala, the Finnish epic, the world egg fell and broke. Its upper part became the vault of heaven, its lower part the earth, the yolk formed the sun, the white the moon, and the fragments of the shells became the stars of heaven.

To ensure fertility in their fields and to produce abundant crops, farmers in Europe and Asia smeared their ploughs with a mixture of eggs, flour, and bread when they did their spring ploughing. Brides in France broke an egg as they entered their new homes after marriage to ensure good fortune in the years ahead. They also believed that the many healing qualities of eggs included: yolks of newly laid eggs beaten in warm water, called hen's milk, should be taken at bedtime to cure a cold; the fine skin inside the shell, beaten and mixed with the white, was excellent for chapped lips; and the shell, burnt and pounded, whitened teeth, and if taken in wine, stopped spitting or the flow of blood.

For centuries bread has been a symbol of rebirth and resurrection, and cross-marked buns are a custom that predates Christianity. In ancient Greece such buns honoured Diana, goddess of the hunt, and the Egyptians ate them to celebrate Isis, the mother goddess.

Stories about eggs and bread are only a small part of the folklore, beliefs, and superstitions involving food, for lamb, pork, hare, fruit, fish, and sweets of all kinds were honoured on pagan tables as spring arrived. It isn't surprising then to learn that these favourite foods were kept on the tables of Christians now celebrating a new feast day.

Christians arriving in British North America brought all their memories and traditions of the foods that were likely prepared and enjoyed before or after they attended their place of worship on this special day. In addition, Lent was now over (that forty days when fasting was expected and practised in most Christian homes). John Lambert gives us a description of a French-Canadian feast in Lower Canada about 1806:

When their long fast in Lent is concluded,
they have their *jours gras* of days of feasting.
Then it is that every production of their farm
is presented for the gratification of their appetites: immense turkey pies; huge joints of pork,
beef and mutton; spacious tureens of soup, or
thick milk; besides fish, fowl, and a plentiful supply of fruit-pies, decorated the board.
Perhaps fifty or a hundred sit down to dinner;
rum is drunk by the half-pint without water;
the tables groan with their load, and the room
resounds with jollity and merriment. No
sooner however does the clash of the knives
and forks cease than the violin strikes up and
the dances commence. Minuets, and a sort of
reel or jig rudely performed to the discordant
scrapings of a couple of vile fiddlers, conclude
the festival or *jours gras*.[1]

As settlers from around the world continued to arrive in
Canada, they brought with them their recipes for their favourite breads for this celebration. Rich in butter, eggs, spices,
honey, dried fruits, nuts, and candied fruit peel, these breads
were perfect symbols of spring, new life, and hope in a new
homeland. At teas, community meals, and other gatherings
new arrivals such as Paska, Babka, Kulich, Panettone, Pretzels

("little arms"), and many more round, braided, tall, and luscious breads were part of the feast.

By the late nineteenth century, the celebrations of Good Friday and Easter were the focus of other community events in many towns and cities in Canada, as announced in the "Local News" column in Elora, Ontario, in 1877:

> The Museum will be open Good Friday afternoon from 1 to 4 o'clock. Something New: An Orange Social will be held in the Methodist Parsonage, on Easter Monday evening. Proceeds to aid the Chandelier Fund. Admission 25 cents each.[2]

In the spirit of other special days, the sending of Easter greetings and small gifts to family and friends was gaining popularity by the end of the century. In 1883, John Young describes and encourages the custom among his readers of *Our Deportment; or the Manners, Conduct and Dress of the Most Refined Society*:

CHRISTMAS AND EASTER CARDS

> A very charming custom that is coming into vogue is the giving or sending of Easter and Christmas cards. These are of such elegant

designs and variety of colours that the stationer takes great pride in decorating his shop windows with them, indeed some of them are so elegant as to resemble oil paintings. Books and other small offerings may accompany cards as tokens of remembrance.[3]

"An Easter to Remember," described by Barbara Parry in the *Farmer's Advocate and Canadian Countryman*, takes us back to the early twentieth century:

> When I was a youngster, Easter was almost as wonderful as Christmas — perhaps more so because it was just our immediate family. My mother always outdid herself for this occasion. Her Easter dinners were something I shall always recall with pleasure. And now for the menu!
>
> Fruit Cocktail, Stewed Chicken with Parsley Dumplings, Candied Sweet Potatoes, Buttered Peas, Carrot Sticks, Celery, Orange Refrigerator Cake, Coffee.[4]

Meanwhile, if you lived in Prince Edward Island and were reading *Mrs. Flynn's Cookbook*, published in 1931, here are her recommendations for your table of celebration:

EASTER DINNER

Cream of Asparagus Soup
Croutons
Curled Celery   Salted Almonds   Olives
Rolls
Fried Fillets of Flounders   Cucumber Sauce
Maryland Chicken and Cream Peas
Mashed Potatoes
Apple and Grape Fruit Salad Garnished with Peppers
Pineapple   Bavarian Cream   Cakes
Assorted Nuts and Raisins
Coffee[5]

15

"Damned Cold Water
Drinking Societies!"

Lips that touch liquor will never touch mine.

— Temperance Movement Slogan

The early days of settlement in Canada were often marred by the use and abuse of alcohol. Many reasons have emerged about its cause, often stressing the nature of a frontier society with families living in isolation who are trying to clear land for farms, build houses in virgin forests, are possessed of no roads, and endure a wildly fluctuating climate. The fertile virgin fields that produced crops beyond anyone's expectations and couldn't be transported to mill or market but could be distilled into whiskey were also blamed.

In addition to all the other reasons proposed, another contributing factor that we should consider was the popularity of "bees" in colonial Canada. The word *bee* comes from Old English and means "a meeting for communal work or amusement." Bees sprang up everywhere as neighbourly gatherings for various kinds of work. For women, quilting bees or preserving bees provided the fellowship and opportunity to gossip and the companionship of other women while accomplishing difficult tasks.

For younger people, apple-paring, pumpkin-drying, or corn-husking bees, where girls and young men worked together, provided an opportunity to socialize and size up who might be a future partner in marriage. Land-clearing, logging, house, church, and school building, or harvesting crops were almost impossible to accomplish alone and became the typical examples of pioneer co-operation. Huge preparations had to be made, for whomever "called the bee" was expected to provide a "spree" as well as return the favour when needed. An early settler in the Peterborough district, Frances Stewart, describes a bee when her new home was built:

> Young ladies came to help with the baking of
> the huge quantities of pies and cakes which
> were served for dinner, in addition to a roast
> pig and boiled leg of mutton, a dish of fish,
> a large cold mutton pie, cold ham and cold

roast mutton, mashed potatoes and beans and
carrots, a large rice pudding, a large bread-
and-butter pudding and currant and goose-
berry tarts, all eaten at noon. Later it began to
rain ... a substantial tea was served soon after,
whereupon dancing commenced until eleven.
A supper almost as substantial as the dinner
was then brought forth, after which dancing
was resumed and continued until one.[1]

As well as food, many bees provided unlimited whiskey
for the workers. Some records tell of as many as eighty gallons
consumed at one bee.[2] Susanna Moodie, another early settler
in the Peterborough area, describes the chaos that resulted at a
logging bee in July 1834:

At dinner time all sat down to the best fare
that could be procured in the bush: pea soup,
legs of pork, venison, eel, and raspberry pies,
garnished with plenty of potatoes, and whiskey to wash them down, besides a large iron
kettle of tea.... While some of the men were
pretty far gone by that time there was nothing particularly objectionable until supper ...
the vicious and drunken stayed to brawl and
fight.... How glad I was when they at last

broke up and we were once more left in peace
to collect the broken glasses and cups and the
scattered fragments of that hateful feast.[3]

Newcomer and author Joseph Pickering tells us that "they
always contrive to have some whiskey at these 'bees' which are
a kind of merrymeeting."[4] Unfortunately, they became much
more than *merrymeetings*, for frequently the men who arrived
to help with the heavy tasks refused to work without getting
whiskey. The story is told of a temperance supporter who
refused to provide liquor at a bee. A group of eight outraged
neighbours pulled down the logs on his barn as fast as they
were put in place.[5]

On average a host could expect to provide a gallon of whiskey for every family that showed up. Every bee had a "grog
boss" who kept the booze flowing to the workers. Drinking
continued throughout meals and into the merrymaking after
the work was completed. Unfortunately, there were many fatal
accidents either at the bees or as a result of the uncontrolled
drinking at them. David Dobie of Ekfrid Township, on the
banks of the Thames River, tells this horrific story

of a group of helpers at a bee on their way
home, when one who had imbibed too freely
refused to go on. He was left to "sleep it off"
in a fence corner. When he failed to return

home by morning his friends searched for
him, found the place where he had slept, and
a few shreds of clothing and body. Wolves
had found him helpless, torn him apart and
feasted on the mangled carcass.[6]

To counteract the growing problem of abundant and cheap
liquor, the first temperance societies were formed in the United
States as early as 1807 in Virginia and 1821 in Massachusetts,
with the movement spreading quickly through the new republic. The first temperance society in British North America seems
to have been in Russelltown in the Eastern Townships of Lower
Canada in 1822, followed by Gloucester, New Brunswick, in
1826; West River, Nova Scotia, and Bedeque County, Prince
Edward Island, in 1827; and Beaver River, Nova Scotia, Bastard
Township, Upper Canada, and Montreal in 1828. So popular
was the movement that by 1832 there were a hundred societies
with ten thousand members in Upper Canada, and in Nova
Scotia eighty societies with thirty thousand members by 1837.[7]
Meetings of the societies featured an opening prayer, an address
or sermon on the evils of intemperance, and after the sermon,
if it wasn't a "teetotal" society, a discussion followed on the mer-
its of total or partial abstinence.

From the beginning the societies were divided on the mer-
its of the "old" and new "pledge." The old pledge was taken
against the indulgence in spirituous liquors, but the use of

wine and beer was allowed. The new pledge was for total abstinence from all alcoholic beverages except for medicinal purposes. This distinction made for three classes of societies: those devoted to total abstinence, those allowing the use of wine and beer, and combination societies with both pledges. A part of the annual meeting in the two last types was devoted to admitting new members and to changing the pledges of those who wished to become teetotalers.

The first total abstinence society in Canada was formed at St. Catharines in the Niagara District on June 15, 1835, when almost forty signatures were obtained. The leaders in the temperance movement soon reached the conclusion that only total abstinence societies could succeed, and by 1840 that type was the most popular. Different types of societies were formed. Separate groups were organized among young people, women, and soldiers. Blacks weren't forgotten, for an African Temperance Society was formed in St. Catharines by 1835.[8] In retrospect it is impossible to judge the success of some of these local societies. They certainly were opposed in many quarters, and Colonel Thomas Talbot described them as mere "damned cold water drinking societies."[9]

The organization of fraternal societies soon followed to assist the multitudes of reformed men to keep their pledges to total abstinence. The Sons of Temperance was started in New York in 1842 and was planted in Quebec, New Brunswick, and Nova Scotia five years later with a phenomenal growth in members.[10] About ten years later the Independent Order of Good Templars was organized in the United States, as well, quickly spreading to Canada under the name British American Order of Good Templars. For sixty years it was the largest temperance organization in the world.

In 1847 the Ladies Total Abstinence Society was formed in Saint John, New Brunswick, and a quarter-century later the Women's Christian Temperance Union emerged. This group was from its inception one of the main factors for the temperance advance in Canada, despite the comments of Colonel Talbot.[11]

Poor roads, difficulties in transportation, and the Canadian climate resulted in inns and taverns being built about every mile on well-travelled routes. These inns also served as gathering places for the settlers, the location for the courts, the headquarters for elections, and every other social occasion such as dances, banquets, and travelling circuses, as well as the meeting places for agricultural societies, the British Constitutional Society, the St. George Society, and many others. Not surprisingly, many early Canadian inns were known for their poor food and were the scene of many drunken brawls, hardly conducive to a good night's sleep.

In Beamsville, Upper Canada, in 1838, Anna Jameson was served "the traveller's fare in Canada — venison steaks and fried fish, coffee, hot cakes, cheese and whisky punch." The landlady gave her a "horrid picture of the prevalence of drunkenness, the vice and curse of this country."[12]

The solution to the problem was the opening of the temperance hotels with their orderly, clean appearance, fine meals, and non-alcoholic beverages. "Temperance Hotel" was prominently displayed on the hotel's exterior, or it was listed as "T.H." in maps and guidebooks to Upper Canada so that this logo reassured the travellers in unknown territory. In ambience the temperance hotels provided a safe haven and a guarantee of quiet. Mary Lundie Duncan writes that:

> In frequenting the temperance houses the traveler is sure of society of one stamp, so that the conversation that he may enter into will be of a correct and very likely of an improving character. The wholesome "click" of ice against water-pitchers has something reassuring in its quiet sound; and the gong, giving forth its musical tone, first in the distant part of the parallelogram, then swelling near till it passes along the gallery where your own chamber is situated, and then again sinking into silence at the further end, summoning all who will to family worship, gives the cheering token that you are in good society. It is very pleasant to meet three or four score of travelers in the saloon by seven in the morning and nine at night to join in a hymn, led

perhaps by a son or daughter of the house accompanied by an organ-toned pianoforte. Then to hear a passage of Holy Writ, read perhaps by the master of the hotel, and to join in a prayer by him if no clergyman be present. How calm and safe the progress of a day so entered upon! And how orderly is such a household, even though it numbers at its noonday meal nearly two hundred guests![13]

Sarsaparilla, a popular beverage, was more than a temperance drink, since it was also acclaimed for its miraculous curative powers. On its front page in December 1849, *The Nova Scotia* had these claims to make about sarsaparilla: "This extract is put up in Quart Bottles.... It cures diseases without vomiting, purging, sickening or debilitating the patient." The boosters of sarsaparilla claimed that it had cured one hundred thousand cases of diseases and that it had saved the lives of fifteen thousand children, made barren women fertile, and restored those who had "excessive indulgence of the passions ... fainting sensations, premature decay and decline." According to the *Dictionary of the English Language* of 1850, sarsaparilla was an abstract of the roots of several species of the genus *Smilax*, native to South America, while wild sarsaparilla is the common name of the genus *Aralia* or ginseng.

Tea and coffee drinking were well established in Upper Canada before the temperance movement started. In 1833 coffee sold for two shillings, nine pence per pound, and tea for one shilling, nine pence per pound (whiskey was three shillings per gallon, and sugar was 30 shillings per hundred pounds as a comparison). Green tea was commonly served at breakfast, though black tea was preferred by British settlers rather than coffee as a beverage with meals. "If tea was not available a substitute of hemlock, hickory or other nauseous vegetables is pressed into service," but these substitutes were never popular.[14]

The usual pattern of dining in Canadian inns and hotels during the heyday of the temperance hotels was with fixed times for meals: 7:30 a.m. breakfast, 1:00 p.m. dinner, and 7:00 p.m. supper. Occasionally, afternoon tea was served, though this was rare in the small inns in the bush. The food on the tables of the temperance hotels wasn't dissimilar to their intemperate counterparts but with an emphasis upon good food in the "plain but orderly dining room where substantial well-cooked, twenty-five-cent dinners were served."[15] Here the guests helped themselves to heaping platters that had been placed on a long table when the guests were seated.

English travellers were amazed by this spread of abundance and the voracious appetites of the Canadians. The fare from the 1830s to the 1870s was ample, hearty, and rich in fat and sugar. Meat was a must three times a day, beginning with "beef-stake" or pork fried in lots of fat and the "never-failing buckwheat cakes." For dinner at noon, the most substantial meal of the day, there were always roasts of beef or pork. Moodie describes an entire roast pig that was placed on the table and carved by one of the guests.[16] Wild game and fowl frequently made their way to the table — venison, ducks, geese, partridge, quail, all roasted, boiled, or stewed. An English traveller thought it was "sacrilege" to use game in a stew but admitted it was good.[17]

The wife of the innkeeper was usually in charge of the kitchen and often ran the inn, as well, if her husband had other work. The equipment was simple: a cook stove in a Toronto inn in the 1840s was sufficient "to boil water, bake bread and cook meat for one hundred persons." The difficulties of transport in Canada precluded importing anything except the bare necessities until the late nineteenth century.

Temperance hotels may have vanished from the Canadian landscape, and we may no longer hear the Cold Water Army singing "Cold water is the drink for me — cold water, cold water is the drink for me," but a mute witness remains. Pure water, plentiful ice, and the strength of the temperance movement contributed to the custom of ice water on the table, and the temperance hotels helped to institutionalize the practice. Water was on the table in the temperance houses by the 1850s, and though these hotels are gone, the ice water remains on the tables in Canadian hotels and restaurants.

16

Mother:
The Hero of the Hearthfire

God could not be everywhere and therefore he made mothers.

— Jewish Saying

From the beginning of time women have appeared to possess miraculous qualities in their ability to produce children, and then from their own bodies to provide them with food. For men in ancient times this must have seemed like an act of magic that was denied to them. Historians believe that it wasn't until the beginning of the Iron Age, about 3,500 years ago, that the role men played in conception was understood.

Mother

The term *Mother Earth* was a logical one, for it was assumed that just as women were the mothers of men, so the earth was the mother of mankind, providing animals for the hunt, wild plants for food, and flowing streams to quench their thirst. In some cultures matriarchal societies developed with the Sacred Mother revered and honoured.

In pre-Christian Europe the coming of spring meant joyful acknowledgement of birth and rebirth, and naturally mothers were recognized as part of this tradition. The coming of Christianity to northern Europe and Great Britain incorporated the old traditions into the new religion, and the fourth Sunday in Lent eventually became known as Mothering Sunday. This, like St. Patrick's Day, was a welcome break from the endless, dreary winter and the forty-day fast that had begun on Ash Wednesday. For families with servants it became customary to send them home for the day so they could honour their own mothers.

One of the traditions popular in England was for children, as they grew older, to make Simnel Cakes to present to their mothers on Mothering Sunday. This is a rich, fruity concoction that shows the marriage between pagan and Christian beliefs. Its name, *simnel*, comes from the Latin *simellus* — a Roman bread made from a fine wheat flour called *simila*, which was eaten regularly at spring fertility rites. This flour was eventually used to make the cake saluting the obvious fertility of motherhood. Eggs, another springtime tradition, were fashioned out of marzipan icing and placed around the cake. First there were supposed to be thirteen marzipan eggs, representing Christ and his disciples. Then there were just twelve. Then Judas was dropped, and the number settled at eleven. We know that this tradition arrived in Canada, for in the twentieth century Michael Brown made a nine-pound Simnel Cake at the Spring Garden Bakery in Halifax that was recorded in the *Guinness Book of World Records* as the largest such cake ever baked.[1]

In those small rural communities that many of our ancestors left for a new life in colonial Canada, Simnel Cakes would have been accepted as a community tradition. Everyone in such villages or towns had watched with interest as each girl or boy grew from birth to an employable or marriageable age and took an interest in their development and welfare.

Like other passages of life, the birth of a child was surrounded by beliefs, superstitions, and traditions. When hospitals were unknown or uncommon, childbirth occurred at home, and many precautions were taken to ensure the safe arrival of a baby. It was often a family member or neighbour who was summoned to act as midwife. To ease the child's arrival she would open all the doors in the house and untie all the knots she could find. In some communities it was believed that the pealing of church bells hastened birth, as well. In many cultural groups it was thought that a child's life, character, and fortunes were determined by the day he or she was born, so ancient rhymes predicted the future:

> Monday's child is fair of face,
> Tuesday's child is full of grace,
> Wednesday's child is full of woe,
> Thursday's child has far to go,
> Friday's child is loving and giving,
> Saturday's child works hard for a living,
> But the child that is born on the "Sabbath Day"
> Is blithe and bonny, good and gay.

By the nineteenth century, there were an incredible number of books, articles, and pamphlets being produced in Canada, the United States, and Great Britain that directed parents on the training of their children. This trend continued in the twentieth century when we find Kate Aitken advising her readers to start preparing their daughters "for her second trade — homemaking" at four years of age by suggesting they "boost her up on the counter, hand her a tea towel, and let her wipe the dishes." Mrs. Aitken gives specific instructions as the girls grow older and recommends a menu for a Mother's Day Supper that a thirteen-year-old could prepare for the family:

MENU FOR MOTHER'S DAY SUPPER

Creamed Chicken and Mushroom
with Toast

Jellied Fruit Dessert   Brown Sugar Cookies

Beverages

By age seventeen, Mrs. Aitken assumed that "this daughter of yours has been taught kitchen management, knows how to conserve movement, has learned food budgeting ... Equally important she has been taught how to set a decorative table and put on it a well-prepared attractive meal."[2]

In the meantime an American nurse and author of "The Battle Hymn of the Republic," Julia Ward Howe, began a movement to implement a Mother's Day for Peace. Her duties during the American Civil War made her determined to put an end to all wars. The first Mother's Day for Peace was held in 1872, seven years after the Civil War.

In 1907 another American, Anna Jarvis of Philadelphia, arranged a service at a local church in memory of her own mother who had died the year before. She asked all those attending to wear a white carnation in memory of a loved one. This custom became so popular that, in 1914, U.S. President Woodrow Wilson proclaimed the second Sunday in May as "a public expression of our love and reverence for the mothers of our country."[3] Canada soon followed suit by adopting the same date for Mother's Day. Girls and boys usually wore red flowers if their mother was living and white flowers if she was deceased. The tradition of making greeting cards or gifts, or preparing breakfast in bed, or afternoon tea, or some other special treat as an expression of love for a mother, continues to this day.

Mother's Day in Canada is usually the day when the christening and the baptism of babies and small children takes place. The ceremony may vary a good deal depending on the cultural group, the practices of the church, or the place of worship of the parents. There are often godparents or sponsors who attend and take an active role in the ceremony. In Newfoundland and Labrador, young people often visit their baptismal sponsors on New Year's Day to receive their blessing and enjoy the traditional cakes, candies, and other treats. Gifts are usually given to the baby in whose honour the guests have attended, and a luncheon often follows, either at the parents' or grandparents' home.

In the weeks leading up to a birth, friends or relatives of an expectant mother may have hosted a baby shower when guests were invited to bring a gift and then enjoy a festive array of finger foods such as tiny sandwiches, relishes, cookies, small cakes, and an assortment of non-alcoholic beverages.

The twentieth century brought a tradition developed in Canada called the Mother and Daughter Tea. These teas were sponsored by churches, Women's Institutes, and schools with home economics departments. Magazines and newspapers gave suggestions about the importance of this event:

"Queen for a day" or an afternoon at least —
when mother dons her best bonnet to attend
your mother-daughter tea. It may be her initial
visit to the home economics department of the
school, and since first impressions are lasting
ones, the tea table must be a thing of beauty.

MOTHER DAUGHTER TEA

Midget Cream Puff Salads
Radish Roses   Pickles
Olives
Tea Time Dainties
Coffee   Tea

Plates of wonderful-looking food surrounding a lovely flower centrepiece will make your
table a thing of beauty.[4]

HEROINE OF THE HEARTHFIRE

She keeps the hearthfire burning, holds
the home together, makes a little sanctuary
of love and faith and comfort for her family in the midst of a hectic, turbulent world.
And always the light of her guidance, the

tenderness of her caring, the warmth of her presence, make bright the lives of those she calls her own. She's the heroine of the hearth-fire and the heart — Mother.[5]

17

Happy Birthday, Queen Victoria

*The important thing is not what they think of me,
but what I think of them.*

— Queen Victoria

Who was this woman, Victoria Alexandria, who had, and still has, such a profound influence on Canadians and our Canadian way of life?

She was born on May 24, 1819, in Kensington Palace to Princess Mary Louise Victoria and Edward, Duke of Kent (after whom Prince Edward Island is named). We know that as a child her nickname was "Drina," she had one hundred and thirty-two dolls, and at a period in history when children and servants were expected to be inaudible and invisible, she often declared "I will be good."

Victoria became queen on June 20, 1837, when her father, Edward, died soon after her birth and her three uncles, George IV, Frederick, Duke of York, and William IV, left no surviving legitimate children. In the sixty-four years of her reign as queen of Canada, queen of the British Empire, and after 1867, empress of India, she left her name or title on more than three hundred places: cities, towns, counties, parks, mountains, islands, lakes, bays, and beaches. In addition, her name graces universities, hospitals, schools, public buildings, a horse race, and at least three hundred streets in Canadian communities.

She chose Ottawa as Canada's capital because she believed it combined more advantages than any other place in the country; suggested the pitcher plant engraved on Newfoundland's penny (later the official flower); donated money to the construction of the Roman Catholic cathedral in St. John's, Newfoundland; and wrapped her own scarf around the bishop of Newfoundland's neck on a cold, damp London day at an audience she granted him. Victoria tried to intervene in the 1837 death sentences of the Upper and Lower Canada rebels but was unsuccessful. However, she did successfully promote the confederation of the provinces in 1867. Ontario took "Loyal it began, loyal it remains" as its motto. Slaves escaping from the United States to Canada on the Underground Railroad sang her praises to the tune of "Old Susannah": "I heard old Queen Victoria say if we would all forsake, / Our native land of slavery and come across the lake, / That she was standing on the shore with arms extended wide, / To give us all a peaceful home beyond the rolling tide. / Farewell, old master, this is enough for me. / I'm going straight to Canada, where coloured men are free."

On her birthday, May 24, 1837, Victoria thanked the First Nations for being allies throughout the years and implemented the giving of presents in recognition of their loyalty to Great Britain and its colonies.[1] Her reign from 1837 to 1901 spanned Canada's birth and adolescence, so we came into being a Victorian nation with Victorian ideals for deference, peace, order, good government, and firm, respected codes of conduct for individuals and society, quite a change from the days of her predecessors, the Georges and William IV, a time of extravagance, excess, and four-bottle men, where judges sat in court in the morning only, while (hopefully) they were still sober.

Victoria's coronation on June 28, 1838, was the social event not only of the season but of the year, with a breakfast for two thousand people following the ceremony, which was produced by Alexis Soyer, one of the many classical French chefs who fled to England after the July 1830 revolution in France. There were many celebrations to mark this occasion. In the new City of Toronto a free public feast was held at Market Square to commemorate her coronation. A whole roast ox, beer, a hundred-pound plum pudding, band music, and fireworks made it the best market day in history.[2]

The new queen's world was a male-dominated society where women couldn't vote and possessed very few legal rights. Husbands controlled not only their wives' estates and investments but also any money they earned. There were serious class distinctions, originally an upper and lower class. However, the middle class or merchant class was growing and looking forward to joining the upper class and being able to fill new and larger homes with servants to confirm its status.

On October 10, 1839, Victoria's cousin Albert, Prince of Saxe Gotha, came to call. Five days later Victoria proposed to him. They were married on February 10, 1840, and again the world celebrated with them. When news reached the colonies (which took several weeks), there was another "ox roasted whole … brought into the centre of Market Square [in Toronto] in procession." The citizens were invited to participate "if clean and if they brought their own eating utensils."[3] Later that year their first child, Victoria, was born. This was a love match, and of course their family grew: Edward, Alice, Alfred, Helena, Louise, Arthur, Leopold, and Beatrice. There was a transformation at court, for it became very respectable, more German than English, with very strict rules of conduct. A national mood of self-conscious piety developed. You were expected to do good to children, animals, poor blacks, and servants. You took your servants to church with you, but of course you didn't sit with them since they were seated in the gallery or the back row. The new merchant class, with its offices, shops, and other commercial establishments, soon developed strict rules of conduct for its employees:

OFFICE STAFF PRACTICES, 1852

1. Godliness, cleanliness, and punctuality are the necessities of a good business.
2. This firm has reduced the hours of work, and the clerical staff will now only have to be present between the hours of 7 a.m. and 6 p.m.
3. Daily prayers will be held each morning in the main office. Clerical staff will be present.
4. Clothing must be of a sober nature. The clerical staff will not disport themselves in raiment of bright colour.
5. Overshoes and topcoats may not be worn in the office but neck scarves and headwear may be worn in inclement weather.
6. A stove is provided for the benefit of the clerical staff. Coal and wood must be kept in the locker; it is recommended that each member of the clerical staff bring 4 lb. of coal each day during cold weather.

7. No member of the clerical staff may leave the room without permission. The calls of nature are permitted and clerical staff may use the garden beyond the second gate. This area must be kept in good order.

8. No talking is allowed during business hours.

9. The craving for tobacco, wines, or spirits is a human weakness and as such is forbidden to all members of the clerical staff.

10. Now that hours of business have been drastically reduced the partaking of food is allowed between 11:30 a.m. and noon, but work will not on any account cease.

11. Members of the clerical staff will provide their own pens.

12. The owners expect a great rise in the output of work to compensate for these near Utopian conditions.[4]

Victoria and Albert set up their home and family as the centre of their world and also established dining and entertaining at home as the model for the nobility, gentry, and rising middle class. Victoria had several homes: the newly finished (and disliked) Buckingham Palace, Osborne House on the Isle of Wight, her beloved Balmoral Castle in the Highlands of Scotland, and Windsor Castle. To follow Victoria's lead, you would attempt to own the largest home possible and staff it with as many servants as possible to augment your place in society. You would have land stewards to manage your estate, rents, and tenants, with support provided by a master of the horse, coachmen, stable boys, grooms, under-coachmen, parks keepers, gamekeepers, gardeners, and yard boys. Indoors you would have housekeepers, cooks or chefs, butlers, gentlemen in waiting, valets, confidential advisers, footmen, under-butlers, hall boys, and foot boys. Below stairs would be the lady's maids, chambermaids, housemaids, laundry maids, dairy maids, maids of all work, scullery maids, and tweenies.

In 1891 there were 1,386,167 females and 58,527 males working in England as indoor servants in private homes. Many of them were between ten and fifteen years of age. The male staff who worked above the stairs wore livery, and we know that Queen Victoria's staff wore the royal scarlet and blue. She employed as her chef Monsieur Ménager, who owned his own London home and arrived each morning in a hansom cab. He was paid £500 a year, while the master chefs under him, one assigned to each dish to be served at a meal and earning £15 a year, would bring the dishes to him for his approval at every stage of their development. Victoria also had an Italian confectioner to prepare the ices, sweets, and desserts that were so popular. After she became empress of India in 1867, she also employed an Indian cook to prepare fresh curries each day. Around this time Empire Cookies made their appearance. A very thin round shortbread cookie was covered with raspberry or strawberry jam. Another thin round cookie with a hole cut in the centre was laid on top of it. The red centre signified England, and the surrounding circle represented the world and the far-flung British Empire.

Queen Victoria's household set the standard to which everyone strived, and the following were the rules for those in service, as described in *The Servant's Behaviour Book*:

1. Never let your voice be heard by the ladies and gentlemen of the house except when necessary, and then as little as possible.

2. Never begin to talk to your mistress, unless it be to deliver a message, or ask a necessary question.

3. Never talk to another servant, or person of your own rank, or to a child, in the presence of your mistress, unless from necessity, and then do it as shortly as possible in a low voice.

4. Never call out from one room to another.

5. Always answer when you receive an order or reproof.

6. Never speak to a lady or gentleman without saying "Sir," "Ma'am," or "Miss," as the case may be.

7. Always stand still and keep your hands before you, or at your sides, when you are speaking or being spoken to.

8. Nursemaids are often encouraged to sing in the nursery; but they should leave off immediately on the entrance of a lady or gentleman.

9. Never take a small thing into the room in your hand. A small thing should be handed on a little tray, silver or not, kept for the purpose.

10. Never make the mistake of going to walk or sit in the garden, as if it were a part of the house belonging to you, as the kitchen and servants' bedrooms.

11. Do not ever choose gay colours or patterns. Not only are such dresses unfit for morning work, after they are a little worn, but they can never look becoming for servants.[5]

Breakfast parties were recommended to the fashionable hostess as being less expensive and very pleasing to guests. The breakfast table was set with matching cloth and napkins with coloured borders, and flowers or a flowering plant graced the centre of the table. Victoria's loyal subjects knew her as a great advocate of porridge for breakfast after her first visit to Scotland and her observations of the ruddy and healthy appearance of Scottish children. When she discovered that their rosy cheeks and healthy bodies could be attributed to porridge, she introduced it to her own children. Everyone else followed suit, and the new breakfast dish spread to the colonies. One of the advantages of porridge was that if it was served as the first course, the cook had time to prepare the many other dishes to follow while the porridge was being consumed. These could include broiled sardines on toast, sweetbreads garnished with French peas, porterhouse steaks, mushrooms, fried oysters, fillet of grouse, Parisienne potatoes, sliced oranges, waffles with maple syrup, sauterne, tea, coffee, chocolate, toast, French rolls.[6]

Dinner was traditionally served at noon or close to it until Victoria came to the throne and began to move it through the afternoon and evening until 8:00 p.m. Two other meals then emerged — lunch and afternoon tea. In comparison to dinner these were relatively informal meals while the rules for dinner were very firm. Invitations were delivered in writing by messenger or personally, and a prompt reply was returned personally or by messenger. Guests didn't know who else had been invited but were safe in the knowledge that other guests would be the same social standing as themselves.

Everyone arrived promptly. The host waited only fifteen minutes and then, in those pre-cocktail days, a ceremonial move to the table began — the host leading the way, escorting the most honoured lady on his left. The other gentlemen followed with the assigned lady (often in order of age), with the hostess bringing up the rear with the gentleman of honour on her right. Napkins were spread across the knees. Ladies removed their gloves, often covering gloves, evening bags, and fans with their napkins, then tucking the two side corners under like lap robes with everything tied in place.

The handwritten or printed menu cards at each place were scanned while waiting for the meal to begin. A typical dinner included a choice of two soups, several fish dishes, various roasted meats and fowl, a selection of vegetables, sweets, desserts, fresh or dried fruits. Each course was accompanied by an appropriate wine, with dessert paired with Madeira. It was Victoria who introduced sorbet before the meat course to cleanse the palette in preparation for it. She also stopped the practice of ladies withdrawing at the end of a meal to the parlour for tea and coffee while the gentlemen remained behind with their port, cigars, walnuts, and conversation, often relieving themselves in the chamber pots under the sideboard.

Victoria never visited Canada. However, her eldest son, Albert Edward, the future King Edward VII, then eighteen years old, embarked on an extensive tour in 1860. Invitations from the Province of Canada (Canada West and East), Nova

Scotia, New Brunswick, Prince Edward Island, Newfoundland, and even the United States brought him on an extensive and exhaustive tour that lasted from July 23 to November 15. Edward was wined and dined and toured on foot, in trains, and in ships. The prince was entertained at balls, concerts, parades, high-wire acts, and levees, and he attended church services and listened to more than three hundred addresses of welcome!

Cookery books in Canada, both handwritten and printed, began to feature recipes honouring Victoria, Albert, and Edward — Prince of Wales Cake, Prince Albert Cake, Queen of Puddings, and Victoria Pudding. The last named continued to be popular for many years:

VICTORIA PUDDING

Three eggs, their weight in butter and flour, 1 good teaspoonful of soda rubbed into the flour, 2 tablespoonfuls brown sugar, 5 table-spoonfuls of jam. Steam two hours.[7]

With the death of Albert in 1861 from typhoid fever, Victoria went into mourning, seldom seen by her subjects except for the celebration of her Golden Jubilee in 1887 and her Diamond Jubilee in 1897. Her death on January 22, 1901, brought an end to her sixty-four-year reign. She continued to have a powerful effect on her loyal followers, with her picture in public buildings, drawing rooms, and even butlers' pantries. Her birthday had first been celebrated in 1845 when the legislators of Canada West declared a holiday. After her death, the government of Prime Minister Wilfred Laurier declared her birthday a national holiday, which it has remained. On that day Canada also celebrates Queen Elizabeth II's birthday, as well (actually April 21). Since 1952, the official Victoria Day has been celebrated on the last Monday before May 25.

Many Canadians look back on the Victorian period with nostalgic affection. However, this period saw the greatest migration the world has ever experienced. Many of our ancestors chose the colonies in preference to the industrialization in England, the land clearances in Scotland, and the Irish potato famine. They came to find their own land, their own freedom, their own destiny. They didn't want to be servants — they wanted to be their own masters. Thank God they did, for otherwise many of us wouldn't be here today.

18

La Fête de St-Jean-Baptiste

*I baptize with water: but there standeth one among you,
whom ye know not; he it is, who coming after me is preferred
before me, whose shoe's latchet I am not worthy to unloose.*

—John 1:26

The celebration of the birthday of St. John the Baptist is on June 24, officially known as Midsummer's Day. It is believed by many historians to have been chosen and sanctified in order to absorb the old pagan festival of the sun into the calendar of the Christian Church's holy days. The ancients believed that June 23, Midsummer's Eve, and June 24, Midsummer's Day, were times of magic. The days had begun to shorten and the nights to lengthen, leading to their beliefs that:

> Then the fairies are abroad, and the witches too. The witches go flying on their broom-sticks, or riding on black cats through the air, to gather on the high hills, there to meet the Devil and swear their allegiance to him. On these high hills they light their fire, and dance around it, keeping their backs to the fire, and their faces turned towards night.[1]

Traditionally, this was the time for herbs, flowers, and other plants that had magic powers to be gathered. These included fernseed to make one invisible and springwort that, if kept in a pocket, prevented injuries from knives or bullets.[2]

The birthday of St. John the Baptist is one of the old-est of the Church's feasts and is sometimes called "Summer Christmas." The Bible describes John the Baptist preaching in the wilderness of Judea with "his raiment of camel's hair and a leathern girdle about his loins; and his meat was locust and wild honey." His message was to announce the coming of the Lord Jesus and to baptize him in the Jordan River.

On the eve of the feast day great bonfires were once lighted as a symbol of the burning and brilliant "light, St. John who identified Jesus in a world of darkness." Although the bonfires had once been part of the pagan solstice celebrations, they were now blessed in John's honour. The pagan beliefs and superstitions about food and drink were forgotten and everyone was encouraged to have picnics and feasts out of doors around the blazing logs.

It may have been Latvia that first decreed a national holiday for this feast, with each man or boy with the name John as the guest of honour. Every house had open house, and the table was set with cold cuts served with grated wild horseradish, bread, butter, honey, and sweet beer. This was a homebrew prepared for all the great Latvian festivals, a combination of barley, rye, hot water, and hops strained through layers of straw. Singing groups went door to door, and housewives treated them to bread and St. John cheese (made with goat's milk), while the men were offered mugs of sweet beer.

In England the tradition developed of newcomers in a community placing small tables at the front of their homes with bread and cheese for passersby. Those who paused to sample were invited indoors, so newcomers quickly made friends with their neighbours![3]

When new arrivals made their homes in Lower Canada, St-Jean-Baptiste became their patron saint, and his feast day was adopted as an official holiday in Quebec. In many homes the traditional *tourtière* was made from a ragout of pork, veal, and beef and enjoyed with root vegetables and white or brown sauce.[4] Traditional bonfires still light the sky, and parades are popular with a float featuring St. Jean as a shepherd boy with a pet lamb at his side. The lamb is woolly white with a ribbon and bow around his neck. There are sports, games, plays, food, and candy.

Remembering John, "whose meat was locusts and honey," an appropriate condiment to have on hand for this day would be Honey Butter, as it can be served with hot buns, toast, or crackers:

HONEY BUTTER

½ cup honey
½ cup butter
juice of ½ lemon

Cream the butter with the honey. Add the lemon juice and beat until a light consistency. Refrigerate in a bowl or a jar until ready to serve.[5]

For children celebrating the day with its parades, games, and a full measure of excitement try:

HONEY COOKIES

2 eggs
1 cup sugar
1 cup honey
1 teaspoon soda
1 tablespoon ginger
1 tablespoon cinnamon
flour to roll

Chill dough before attempting to roll very thin and cut. These can be cut into shapes to suit the celebration — small boys, or lambs, or whatever your imagination guides your hand to do. Use a pancake turner to lift the cookies onto the greased cookie sheet. Place in 350-degree oven for about 10 minutes, as these cookies burn very easily. They are best made 2 or 3 days in advance of the festivities.[6]

Because of the coincidence of dates, we might find several different celebrations in progress at this time. For example, if we were in Newfoundland, Discovery Day would be remembered as the day the explorer John Cabot sailed into St. John's harbour on the eve of St. John's Day, 1497.

The ancient celebration of Midsummer's Day or summer solstice survived the journey across the ocean and is still honoured among Canadians of Finnish, Norwegian, and Swedish ancestry, and is often celebrated on the Saturday closest to June 24. Special treats are prepared and brought to the festivities such as Norwegian Fattigmand:

> 6 egg yolks
> 1 tablespoon melted butter
> ½ teaspoon salt
> 3 scant cups flour
> 6 tablespoons sweet cream
> ⅛ tablespoon ground cardamom
> 4 tablespoons sugar

> Beat egg yolks well, add sugar and mix well. Add the melted butter and the rest of the ingredients. Roll *very* thin. Cut in diamond shapes. Make a straight cut in the centre of each diamond. Pull the two ends through the hole. Fry in deep fat at 370 degrees for 2 or 3 minutes or until a golden brown. Dust with powdered sugar.[7]

This is the occasion for picnics, bonfires, concerts, storytelling, and dancing. At Swedish festivals a pole is erected, similar to a maypole, as the centrepiece for the dances. The festival meal usually features salmon and new potatoes, with strawberries for dessert, and a cookie or small cake to serve with them. Among Swedish Canadians in Manitoba a favourite sweet was, and is, Pepparkakor, or Ginger Snaps. They are made and enjoyed at many special events and can be rolled and cut into fancy shapes in honour of the occasion:

PEPPARKAKOR

⅔ cup brown or white sugar
⅔ cup dark syrup
1 teaspoon ginger
1 teaspoon cinnamon
½ teaspoon cloves
¾ tablespoon baking soda
⅔ cup butter
1 cup flour
1 large egg

Heat sugar, syrup, and spices to boiling point. Add baking soda and mixture to butter in a large bowl. Stir until butter melts. Add egg, then sifted flour and blend thoroughly. Knead on baking board; chill. Roll out and cut in fancy shapes. Place on greased baking sheet and bake in 325-degree oven for 8 to 10 minutes.[8]

19

Dominion Day

The wholesome sea is at her gates,
Her gates both east and west.

— John A. Ritchie, "There Is a Land"

On July 1, 1867, the British North America Act united the Provinces of Canada, Nova Scotia, and New Brunswick into one dominion. There had been many battles, including what to name this union. The Kingdom of Canada was finally denied, for fear of angering the United States, which had left one kingdom and wouldn't want to have another as its neighbour. Where was the capital to be? Queen Victoria chose the lumber town of Ottawa to the dismay of many other contenders. Almost immediately Nova Scotia wanted to withdraw, while Newfoundland and Prince Edward Island refused to join. West of Ontario stretched a vast, mysterious land, home of the First Nations, Métis, fur traders, and a few brave settlers. Rupert's Land reached to the Pacific Ocean, and the Hudson's Bay Company held the privileges of fur trade and government, granted by its charter of 1670 to "The Governor and Company of Adventurers of England trading into Hudson's Bay."

Despite insurmountable odds, the political leaders of the day had wined and dined one another, were wined and dined in return, compromised some of their dreams and ambitions, and finally emerged with a new system of government. George-Étienne Cartier, the French-Canadian leader, proclaimed "In our confederation there will be Catholics and Protestants, English, French, Irish and Scotch, and each by its efforts and success will add to the prosperity of The Dominion, to the glory of the new confederation. We are of different races, not to quarrel, but to work together for the common welfare."[1]

How did Canadians react to the first Dominion Day, the day that had been so long in coming? On July 12, 1867, the *Ottawa Citizen* reported:

> Confederation Day appears to have been generally well-observed throughout the Dominion. But in Nova Scotia, in the

> strongholds of anti-Unionism, the day passed over without jubilation. This is, of course, no more than we might have predicted, for weeks ago the anti-Confederation journals recommended that the day be devoted to fastings and humiliation …

They may have fasted in Nova Scotia, but other communities were more fortunate. The *Globe* of Toronto, whose owner and editor George Brown had formed a coalition with John A. Macdonald and Cartier to realize the union, featured the good news as the front-page story on July 1:

> At 6 p.m. an immense ox will be roasted…. The roasting will occupy a large portion of the day and the meat will afterwards be distributed among the poor of the city…. On the roofs of houses and elsewhere flag poles were hoisted … a Grand Review of her Majesty's Troops … a grand Balloon Ascension … concerts were given…. A grand celebration took place at the Horticultural Gardens … brilliantly lighted, and a large tent set up for refreshments of strawberries, ice cream, etc. … Tickets were twenty-five cents, children's tickets ten cents.[2]

The *Evening Times* of Hamilton described the celebrations that were to take place there in the June 29 edition: "All Highlanders are requested to assemble in front of the City Hall on Monday, July 1 at nine a.m. to join in the Confederate Procession headed by the Pipers." This edition assured its readers that "The arrangements seem to be complete, and every indication promises one of the most enthusiastic and imposing demonstrations to mark the dawning era of the new Dominion." The roar of artillery and the ringing of bells were promised for midnight and again for 6:00 a.m.! How did Hamiltonians enjoy the day? The *Toronto Leader* reported on July 3, 1867, on the aftermath of the Dominion Day festivities in Hamilton:

> The city has shaken down again into its staid old habits. There was a remarkable absence of drunkenness on Dominion Day, and the behaviour of the people generally was worthy of all praise. It appeared to be reserved for the race course to show the worst example, and strangely enough although no liquor tents were on the ground, there was more than the usual amount of drunkenness. The great cry was for places of refreshment, and the dust being heavy it was disagreeable — nothing, not even water to quench the

thirst; yet there were many drunken persons abroad, and no less than six fights occurred the first day.[3]

In subsequent years refreshments, including food and beverages, became popular whether the Dominion Day festivities consisted of bands, parades, a sports day, a political picnic, or an outing organized by a local church or benevolent organization. The first political picnic was held on Dominion Day in 1876 in Uxbridge, Ontario, and the menu was a stunning array of foods. That picnic is fully detailed in Chapter 21, "Pic-Nics, Pleasure Parties, and Garden Parties," of this book. Excursions to rivers, lakes, and favourite beauty spots became increasingly popular with family groups. Cookery books such as the *Canadian Cook Book* suggested the contents for a Box Pic-Nics, including Ham Rolls, tomatoes, pickles, Date Cake, chocolate milk or Pea Soup (in a Thermos), Chicken Salad Sandwiches, celery, olives, Lemon Butter Tarts, and ginger ale. A Basket Picnic could include Sliced Veal Loaf, Chili Sauce, Potato Salad, celery, olives, pineapple, strawberries, Cup Cakes, tea, coffee, or cocoa (in a Thermos).[4]

Hotels and restaurants offered special menus on this special day:

SUPPER MENU

Regina Café
Dawson City, Yukon
Dominion Day, 1898
Consommé à la Jardinière
Rockport Oysters, Raw

Gherkins   Piccalilli

Lobster Cutlets, à la Newberg
Pickled English Walnuts
Chicken Salad en Mayonnaise
Broiled Moose Chops aux Champignons
Cold Tongue, Roast Beef, Boiled Ham
Bengal Club Chutney
Saratoga Chips
Assorted Cakes and Jellies

Pears   Peaches

Edam Cheese
Coffee[5]

20

Feasts of the Fur Traders

*They might in the future more than ever before
engage in hunting beavers.*

— Samuel de Champlain

The beaver is celebrated as a national symbol on stamps, coins, and emblems. Hundreds of Canadian lakes, towns, rivers, and mountains bear its name, and it has influenced Canadian history more than any other animal.

Long before the arrival of newcomers, the First Nations trapped beaver for both fur and food. The pelts were bartered with other nations on the long trade route that stretched from the Gulf of Mexico to Hudson Bay. They considered the meat and every part of the animal important: cooked beaver tail was a special treat, fat was skimmed off and used for cooking and medicines, and teeth and claws were incorporated into ceremonial wear. Castoreum, a bitter orange-brown substance from the musk gland of the beaver, made a powerful medicine against headaches, reduced fevers, and eased aching joints.[1]

For early newcomers like the French traders and fishermen on the East Coast, beaver pelts were much in demand. In Europe the nobility demanded fine furs for robes, jackets, capes, and muffs, and gentlemen who could afford a fine felt hat insisted that it be made of the soft downy undercoat of the beaver. As European beavers had been trapped out, it was imperative that a fresh source be found, and in the Far Northwest of what would become Canada were the finest pelts in the world.

Two young Frenchmen, Médard Chouart, Sieur des Groseilliers, and Pierre-Esprit Radisson, realized the fortune to be made in the trade. They had both come to New France as young men and had worked and travelled in the St. Lawrence region and beyond as explorers, coureurs de bois, and fur traders among the Huron, Cree, and Sioux Nations. The two Frenchmen realized the untold wealth in furs to be found in the forests surrounding the "Bay of the North" (Hudson Bay) and lobbied in the New and Old Worlds for permission to trade in the region. Finally on May 2, 1670, King Charles II of Great Britain granted his cousin Prince Rupert a royal charter that gave trading rights to the area known as Rupert's Land under the name "The Governor and Company of Adventurers of England trading into Hudson's Bay." No one at that time knew the size of the land mass involved (it was actually 40 percent of modern-day Canada and some territory that is now part of the United States), but the coveted trading rights were for furs, particularly beaver pelts. A few months later Radisson and Groseilliers were on-site and celebrating:

> 25 being Christmas, wee made merry remembering our Friends in England having for Liquor Brandy and strong beer and for Food plenty of Partridges and Venison besides what ye shipps provisions afforded.

This description of Christmas dinner in Canada was fortunately recorded by a new Hudson's Bay Company fur trader, Thomas Gorst, in his journal in 1670. The guests seated at the table in the newly constructed Charles Fort (later called Rupert's House and still later Fort Rupert) included Governor Charles Bayley, Groseilliers, Radisson, and Captain Zacharidh Gillam. The ships *Wivenhoe* and *Prince Rupert* were anchored nearby in James Bay.

Free traders (as the competitors of the Hudson's Bay Company were called) became involved in this lucrative business, and many combined forces by forming partnerships and companies, but it was the North West Company that for many years challenged the powerful Hudson's Bay Company and its decision to build its forts around the bay and let the First Nations come to it. The North West Company realized the importance of building trading posts in the interior of the country where the First Nations lived, trapped, and hunted and the importance of adequately provisioning the men involved in the trade and not leaving their survival and the survival of the business to chance.

To accomplish this the North West Company formed one of the most innovative partnerships ever seen in Canada, including an unlikely combination of Scottish and English merchants, French-Canadian voyageurs, First Nations guides, canoe-makers, advisers, suppliers of survival foods, Métis (children of a mixed marriage between newcomers and First Nations parents), labourers, trappers, traders, and voyageurs. This was a partnership that solved the slow, complicated business of buying or bartering for furs from the First Nations in the northwestern regions of Canada and moving them to ships on the East Coast where they were transshipped to markets overseas. The North West Company developed and maintained a long supply route that stretched from present-day Montreal to the Pacific Ocean, with an inland headquarters between the two.

The first inland headquarters for the North West Company was built at Grand Portage. When the boundary between the newborn United States and the British possessions in North America was redrawn by the Treaty of Versailles in 1785, the headquarters was moved to Fort William (now Thunder Bay) on the north shore of Lake Superior. Fort William became the transshipping centre, with forty-two buildings set in a rectangle and its own farm adjoining the fort to provide provisions such as grain, herbs, fresh vegetables, milk, and meat for the regular staff and the Rendezvous held there annually. The land behind the fort and on both sides of it was cleared and under tillage. Barley, peas, oats, Indian corn, potatoes, and other grains and vegetables were grown there. Seven horses, thirty-two cows and bulls, and a large number of sheep were kept on the farm, as well.[2]

How did this unique system work? To overcome the short summers and long winters in Canada, many of the partners of the company wintered in Montreal, assembling the trade goods, supervising the warehouses along the St. Lawrence River, and preparing for the year ahead. The rest of the partners manned the inland posts in the West and the Far Northwest, trading and bartering directly with the First Nations for the pelts. They, too, were getting ready for the year ahead. As soon as the ice was gone from the lakes and rivers, both groups started for Fort William. The inland traders used small *canots du nord* that could be paddled by six men, could be carried over a portage by two people, and could hold two tons of pelts and provisions for the thousand-mile journey. The Montreal merchants utilized Montreal canoes, or *canots du maître*, which were large freight canoes that held four tons of freight and required ten French-Canadian or Métis voyageurs each as paddlers to cover approximately the same distance.

They [the canoes] reached lengths of forty feet, with a six-foot beam and a depth of two feet. The bow and stern curved upwards, often painted with animals and other designs. They weighed only five hundred pounds but they could carry as many as sixty men or fifty barrels of flour. They could be manufactured from cedar and pine and birch bark for as little as fifty dollars and would last for five or six years. First time travellers blanched when they saw their intended craft loaded to the gunwales perhaps a scant six inches from the water, but the Nor'westers calculated losses on voyages as low as one-half percent.

The canoe fleet carried a mess tent, 30 feet by 15 feet, and a separate sleeping tent and comfortable bed for each partner, carpets for their feet, beaver robes for their knees. The transport canoes went on ahead so that when the gentlemen reached the selected site for the night, a great fire was leaping, meat was sizzling, and the wine bottles were uncorked.[3]

Washington Irving, one of the guests of the North West Company, described the journey from Montreal:

They ascended the river in great state, like sovereigns making a progress, or rather like Highland chieftains navigating their subject lakes. They were wrapped in rich furs, their huge canoes freighted with every convenience and luxury, and manned by Canadian voyageurs, as obedient as Highland clansmen. They carried up with them cooks and bakers, together with delicacies of every kind, and abundances of choice wines for the banquets which attended this great convocation. Happy were they, too, if they could meet with some distinguished stranger; above all, some titled member of British nobility, to accompany them on this stately occasion, and grace their high solemnities.[4]

The Nor'westers coming to Fort William from the inland posts also had to provision their teams. They soon learned that dried meat and fish, berries and greens from the forest, all took space in the canoes and precious time could be wasted hunting and fishing. The First Nations introduced the newcomers to pemmican, made from dried buffalo, elk, or deer meat, pounded into a powder, mixed with dried berries, and packed into a leather bag sealed with grease. Light, durable, and highly nourishing, the bags were easily stored in a canoe, thus pemmican became the staple diet of the canoeman. Small amounts of pemmican replaced large amounts of regular food, freeing up precious time and space to carry more furs and more trade goods in both directions.

> Pemmican was used on voyages in the far interior. This was kind of pressed buffalo meat, pounded fine, to which hot grease was added, and the whole left to form a mould in a bag of buffalo skin. When made properly, pemmican would remain edible for more than one season. Its small bulk and great nutritional value made it highly esteemed by all voyageurs. From it they made a dish called "Rubbaboo" … it is a favourite dish with the northern voyageurs, when they could get it. It consists simply of pemmican made into a kind of soup by boiling water. Flour is added when it can be obtained, and it is generally considered more palatable with a little sugar.[5]

In July the two groups began to assemble at the inland headquarters — the fur brigades from the West and the merchant partners from the East. It isn't surprising that the annual Rendezvous became a legendary time of feasting and celebration. The population of Fort William grew to about two thousand persons (at the same time the population of York, the capital of Upper Canada, was about six hundred) and included the English and Scottish merchants and their clerks, the French-Canadian and Métis canoemen, the men and women of the First Nations who were guides, advisers, and providers of specialized needs such as survival foods for the chain of forts and posts stretching into the interior.

During the month of the Rendezvous, dignity appears to have been set aside once the sun began to set. Days were spent in the committee house at meetings where the business of the trade was carried out in great secrecy, but the nights were spent dining and roistering in the Great Hall. Dinners of

> buffalo tongue and hump that had been either smoked or salted, thirty pounds of lake trout and whitefish that could be netted at the gates to the Fort, venison, wild duck, geese, partridge and beaver tails would be augmented with confectioner's delicacies that had been packed all the way from Montreal in those great canoes. They drank the wines of France and Portugal, whiskies from Scotland and the Canadas, rum by the hogshead and, on occasion, finest champagne.[6]

Traditionally, five toasts honoured the fur trade, and these were given in the following order: Mary, the Mother of all Saints; the king; the fur trade and all its branches; the voyageurs, their wives, and their children; and absent brethren. When the dinner and toasts were finished, the Great Hall witnessed one of the sights of the ages:

> With the ten gallon kegs of rum running low and dawn fingering the windows of the Great Hall to find the partners of the North West Company, names that mark and brighten the map of Canada, leaping on benches, chairs, and oaken wine barrels to "shoot the rapids" from the tilted tables to the floor, and singing the songs of home. Mounting broad bladed paddles, the gentlemen in knee breeches and silver buckled shoes pounded around the hall in impromptu races, shoving boisterously, piling up at the corners, breaking off only to down another brimming bumper [of spirits].[7]

The Rendezvous was soon over, and by August 1 both groups left for home so they wouldn't be caught on the frozen waterways.

Fine dinners weren't just enjoyed at the inland headquarters at the time of the Rendezvous, but at other fur-trading forts, as well. An account of dinner at Fort Vancouver, a North West Company post on the Pacific Slopes that the company firmly controlled (stretching from San Francisco to the Alaska border), finds Governor (Dr. John) McLoughlin, who had served at Fort William, presiding at table:

> At the end of a table twenty feet in length stands Governor McLoughlin (known as the father of Oregon) directing guests and gentlemen from neighbouring posts to their places, and chief traders, the physician, clerks and the farmer slide respectfully to their places, at distances from the governor corresponding to the dignity of their rank. Thanks are given to God, and all are seated. Roast beef and pork, boiled mutton, baked salmon, boiled ham, beets, carrots, turnips, cabbage and potatoes, and wheaten bread, are tastefully distributed over the table among a dinner set of elegant Queen's Ware, furnished with glittering glasses and decanters of various coloured Italian wines.[8]

For the partners who were returning from Fort William to their comfortable homes and families in Montreal to spend the winter, there was the fellowship and feasting of the Beaver

Club to look forward to. The Beaver Club was founded in February 1785 with nineteen members, all of whom had explored the Northwest. The object of the club was to

> bring together at stated periods during the winter season, a set of men highly respectable in society who had passed their best days in a savage country and had encountered the difficulties and dangers incident to a pursuit peculiar to the fur trade of Canada.[9]

Despite this restriction, an additional nineteen members had been accepted by 1803.

The club didn't have its own headquarters but met every fortnight from December to April in one of Montreal's famous eating establishments. It did have its own china, crystal, and plate marked with its insignia. At the meetings the members themselves had to wear the club's insignia if they wanted to avoid a fine. This was a gold medal bearing the words "Beaver Club of Montreal instituted in 1785" with a beaver gnawing the foot of a tree and the inscription "Industry and Perseverance." The reverse carried the name of the member, the date of his first voyage of exploration, and a canoe with three passengers in top hats being guided through rapids by canoemen with the motto "Fortitude in distress."[10]

Colonel Landman, a guest of Sir Alexander Mackenzie and William McGillivray, provides a vivid description of one of the Beaver Club's dinners that lasted twelve hours:

> At this time, dinner was at four o'clock and after having lowered a reasonable quantity of wine, say a bottle each, the married men withdrew, leaving a dozen of us to drink to their health. Accordingly, we were able to behave like real Scottish Highlanders and by four in the morning we had all attained such a degree of perfection that we could utter a war cry as well as Mackenzie and McGillivray. We were all drunk like fish, and all of us thought we could dance on the table without disarranging a single one of the decanters, glasses or plates with which it was covered.
>
> But on attempting this experiment, we found that we were suffering from a delusion and wound up by breaking all the plates, glasses and bottles and demolishing the table itself; worse that that, there were bruises and scratches, more or less serious on the heads and hands of everyone in the group.... It was told to me later that during our carouse 120 bottles of wine had been

drunk, but I think a good part of it had been spilled.[11]

Other guests confirm Landman's description:

> They served bear meat, beaver, pemmican and venison in the same way as in trading posts to the accompaniment of songs and dances during the events; and when wine had produced the sought-for degree of gaiety in the wee hours of the morning, the trading partners, dealers and merchants re-enacted the "grand voyage" to the Rendezvous in full sight of the waiters or voyageurs who had obtained permission to attend. For this purpose, they sat one behind another on a rich carpet, each equipping himself with a poker, tongs, a sword or walking stick in place of a paddle and roared out such *voyageurs'* songs as *Malbrouck* or *A la Claire Fontaine*, meanwhile paddling with as much steadiness as their strained nerves would permit.[12]

In 1821 the Hudson's Bay Company and the North West Company amalgamated, but fine dinners, feasts, and celebrations continued in the fur-trading forts. Paul Kane had his Christmas dinner in 1847 at Fort Edmonton and left this record:

> About two o'clock we sat down to dinner. Our party consisted of Mr. Harriett, the Chief, and three clerks, Mr. Thebo [Thibault], the Roman Catholic missionary from Manitou Lake about thirty miles off, Mr. Rundell [Rundle], the Wesleyan missionary who resided within the picket, and myself ...
>
> The dining-hall in which we assembled was the largest room in the fort, probably about fifty by twenty-five feet, well warmed by large fires, which are scarcely ever allowed to go out. The walls and ceilings are boarded, as plastering is not used, there being no limestone within reach; but these boards are painted in a style of the most startling bar-baric gaudiness, and the ceiling filled with centre-pieces of fantastic gift scrolls, making altogether a saloon which the Indians always looked upon with awe and wonder ... no tablecloth shed its snowy whiteness over the board; no silver candelabra or gaudy china interfered with its simple magnificence. The bright tin plates and dishes reflected jolly

faces and burnished gold can give no truer zest to a feast.

At the head, before Mr. Harriett, was a large dish of boiled buffalo-hump; at the foot smoked a boiled buffalo calf. Start not, gentle reader, the calf is very small, and is taken from the cow by Caesarean operation long before it obtains its full growth. This, boiled whole is one of the most esteemed dishes amongst the epicures of the interior. My pleasing duty was to help a dish of mouffle, or dried moose nose; the gentleman on my left distributed, with graceful impartiality, the whitefish, delicately browned in buffalo marrow. The worthy priest helped the buffalo tongue, whilst Mr. Rundell cut up the beavers' tails. Nor was the other gentleman left unemployed, as all his spare time was occupied dissecting a roast wild goose. The centre of the table was graced with piles of potatoes, turnips, and bread ... such was our jolly Christmas dinner at Edmonton; and long will it remain in my memory.

In the evening, the hall was prepared for the dance.... The dancing was most picturesque, and almost all joined in it. Occasionally

> I, among the rest, led out a young Cree squaw,
> who sported enough beads round her neck
> to have made a pedlar's fortune, and having
> led her into the centre of the room, I danced
> round her with all the agility I was capable
> of exhibiting, to some Highland-reel tune
> which the fiddler played with great vigour,
> whilst my partner with grave face kept jump-
> ing up and down, both feet off the ground at
> once, as only an Indian can dance.[13]

The *Montreal Daily Star* published a photograph and an article by A.A. Chesterfield in 1910 entitled "New Year's in the Far North." Chesterfield was a professional photographer working in Montreal when, between 1901 and 1904, he was employed by the Hudson's Bay Company as a fur trader in the District of Ungava. His article describes the northern custom of breaking the monotony of winter with a period of holiday revelry from Christmas Eve until January 6. The highlight of the holiday occurred on New Year's Day when, as Chesterfield writes,

> the servants and engages, dressed in the best
> the store will furnish, proceed to the factor's
> house in order to wish him a Happy New
> Year. The greeting, and future prosperity, is

the toast which is given with the drinking of one glass of wine. In replying the factor invites them all to dinner.

At one, dinner is served in the mess-room. Tables have been laid to accommodate all who are engaged at the fort, from store-man to chore boy. The tables fairly groan with the weight of venison, wild geese, and plum puddings, and the factor's guests are those who will do full justice to the fare. It is the greatest meal of the year at a fur trade post, and the host sees that all thoroughly enjoy themselves.[14]

What remains of these great fur-trading empires and the feasts many of their partners and participants enjoyed?

The Beaver Club ceased to exist in 1817, but it was resurrected in the twentieth century by the Queen Elizabeth Hotel in Montreal. It now has over nine hundred members around the world who, once a year, dine on a five-course dinner with appropriate wine. Each course is paraded through the club led by costumed coureurs de bois, voyageurs, musicians, and Natives from the Kahnawake First Nation. Now, as then, five toasts are proposed — to the Mother of All Saints, the queen, the fur trade in all its branches, the women and children of the fur trade, and absent brethren.

Feasts of the Fur Traders

Beaver hats have been forgotten by the fashion world and fur-trading empires are a thing of the past, but once a year hundreds of men and women still gather to pay tribute to an unlikely team of men and women who ruthlessly pursued a small animal across this continent, and in doing so, confirmed the size, complexity, and diversity of Canada. Their success depended on their food supplies and the strength, skill, and stamina of a chain of men stretched across the continent. They came from different origins, languages, cultures, and standards, but they found a common cause and became legends in their own time.

21

Pic-Nics, Pleasure Parties,
and Garden Parties

*Even the inexperienced hostess need only supply "a green lawn,
a few trees, a fine day and something to eat."*

— Maude C. Cooke

I t may have been the French who first described "a meal
taken out of doors and away from home, often without
benefit of tables, chairs, or other amenities" with the single
word *piquenique*. By 1748 the word *picnic* was being used to
describe "a social entertainment at which every person contributed food to a common table," and in Great Britain and
Europe this event was often held indoors.

Not everyone was enthusiastic about picnics, as the *Lady's
Book* of 1833 tells us:

> There is a species of entertainment peculiar to
> our islands, called in Wales "grass parties," in
> Jersey "milk parties," and at Greenwich and
> Richmond "pic-nics": they are days devoted
> to all those inconveniences which at less-
> favoured periods would, to use an expressive
> Irishism, "set you mad." You give up the com-
> forts of civilized life — tables and chairs are
> *de trop* — one glass does the work of many —
> and your dinner is spread on the grass, for the
> benefit of the ants, earwigs, and other insects.

We have ample proof that these "grass parties" or "pic-nics" contained little pleasure with a first-hand account by a gentle-man who attended "A Pleasure Party in the Highlands" that had taken place on September 18, 1831, and also published in the *Lady's Book* in November 1833:

> The party consisted of the two elder Miss
> Gordons, my respected aunts; the four juve-
> nile Miss Gordons; my active, early rising,
> indefatigable cousins; three Miss Campbells
> from Castle Craig; one Mr. Campbell from
> ditto; Miss Delauny an Irish heiress, also from
> the Castle; and a gaunt high-cheeked indi-
> vidual, whose sex seemed at first sufficiently

doubtful to afford a ray of hope that Mr. Campbell and myself were not the only gentlemen to a party of nine ladies ...

While Miss Delauny was protesting against being obliged to walk, I took a peep into the hampers, or rather creels, which were slung across the smaller of the two little rough Shetland ponies who were to carry our food. I looked and lo! a little bag of pepper, a larger one of salt, a roll of soft butter, done up in a cabbage leaf, and again — carefully enclosed in a fragment of the last *Perth Courier*, an enormous piece of hard, poor, greenish, whitish cheese, two heavy bannocks of barley meal, a bag, containing four sea biscuits, and one little sweet biscuit, remaining from a case of Leman's, a piece of mutton, composing six scraggy cutlets, three knives, four forks, some flour, and a note, containing the following memorandum, written by the stay-at-home to the pleasuring aunts: "The sweet biscuit is for Miss Delauny, and a knife and fork for ditto, a cutlet and every thing comfortable; the other biscuits for the Miss Campbells. No bread in the house. The men of course, will shoot birds enough to make a good dinner, and no want." ...

> At length it was over: we had made the most uncomfortable meal we could hope to eat in the course of our lives, in the most uncomfortable manner; and we rose to return homewards.

With memories like those it is amazing that picnics for any and every conceivable reason became popular in Canada. The tradition may evolve from our Canadian ancestors' need to cook over open fires, to eat on the move, and to organize large group meals out of doors at the time of harvest, for work bees of all kinds, and for the celebration of special occasions. We can only guess how much this trend was influenced by some of our more famous residents and authors such as Elizabeth Simcoe, wife of the first lieutenant governor of Upper Canada, who continually dined and entertained "on the pretty green bank, in an arbour of oak boughs, by the falls" and other outdoor locations.

Joseph Willcocks, recently arrived from Ireland and later to become Sheriff Willcocks, described in his *Memorandum and Letter Book* an outing near York, Upper Canada, on September 18, 1800:

> I went to the Humber on a pleasure party with Mr. and Miss Russell, Mr. and Miss Willcocks's Mr. Weeks and Doctor Baldwin. We left York

at 10 o'clock and reach'd the Humber in Mr.
Jarvis's Boat at half past 12. Walked about for
an hour and dined at half past 1. We had for
Dinner a piece of Cold Roast Beef, Cold ham,
cold chicken and hot stewed Wild Ducks. We
all arrived safe at home at 5 o'clock in the
Evening ...[1]

Picnics were organized for many reasons: as simple family outings; for family reunions; to complement a parade, regatta, or local festival; or to celebrate special days such as Queen Victoria's birthday. Meadows, parks, churchyards, cemeteries, and town squares were all popular destinations for those who couldn't reach a river or lake easily. Ambitious families and organized groups travelled to spectacular scenic locations such as Niagara Falls for their pleasure parties. One observer at the falls describes such a party in the nineteenth century: "Not far from where I stood, the members of a picnic party were flirting and laughing hilariously, throwing chicken bones and peach stones over the cliff, drinking champagne and soda water."

As picnics became more numerous, everyone tried to capitalize on their popularity and natural charm, and we find that politicians used them to reach their voters, churches and Sunday Schools sponsored them for the edification of their members and adherents, schools featured them with work parties for Arbour Days, fraternal and loyal order lodges twinned them with their parades, and entrepreneurs adopted them for the profits that might be realized by combining them with excursion trains and boats on public holidays. These were all grand occasions, usually attracting large crowds as described in the *Toronto Mail* in 1876 and hosted by the Conservative Party:

> The Toronto excursionists, numbered three or four hundred, about fifty of whom were ladies. The excursion party was conveyed to Uxbridge by a special train on the Toronto and Nipissing railway. The train reached Uxbridge about eleven o'clock, and the party was met at the station by an immense concourse of people, accompanied by the Markham brass band and another. A Procession was formed which preceded by the bands moved through the village to a beautiful grove of noble elms, called Elgin Park. On the way there the procession passed under three triumphal arches, on the first of which displayed the word "WELCOME." In the grove a large number of long tables were laden with succulent turkeys, chickens and geese, roast ducks with wild rice stuffing, garnished tongues, aspic hams, huge roasts, pigeon pastries, giblet pies, sausage smoked in maple syrup, roasted pig tails and

black pudding. There were pickled peaches and pears, sweet mustard pickles, an old settler's "secret" pepper relish, piccalilli and all sorts of breads — a pumpkin loaf served with slathers of freshly churned butter, corn and blueberry muffins, hoe and ash cakes and still hot biscuits. Desserts included cakes such as tipsy, pound, cheese and Huronia maple layer; charlotte russe, flummery and varieties of pies — shoo-fly, honey, rhubarb and mince. Sweet pudding with dried plums competed with Indian pudding, *schnitz* and *knepp* and raised doughnuts. Huge bowls of strawberries, blackberries and currants disappeared along with toppings of thick rich cream. For those who could handle more there were Northern Spy, Royal Russet, and Canadian Nonesuch apples, homemade candy kisses and cheeses in great variety. There was a constant refilling of great pitchers of iced lemonade, berry cordials, cider, domestic champagne and dandelion wine.[2]

In those long-ago days before paper serviettes and plates, and plastic utensils of all kinds, the task of packing for even the simplest picnic was enormous, for it would involve taking the table linens, silverware and china, glassware and teapots, in addition to all the viands and accoutrements that Victorian protocol demanded in presenting the indoors outdoors.

The menus described by the authors of the nineteenth century tend to overwhelm us, for they included roasted fowls, roasted meats, hams, tarts (pies to us) of all kinds of fruit, moulded jellies of various sorts, breads, fruit such as melon, and much more. Not only did the hostess undertake this mammoth task of organization of the food but she had to think about who was to be invited and when the handwritten invitations should be hand-delivered. The compatibility and suitability of the guests was paramount, for again the social leaders warned the unwary hostess: "The mistakes of bringing the wrong people together, of placing them without regard for individual tastes of the vehicles used, or having too many of one sex in the party. At a picnic there is no get-away for any-one, as there is at an evening party or an 'at home.'"

By the early twentieth century, commercial firms were sponsoring picnics for their employees and their families as a reward and recognition of their commitment to their job. Typical of this trend was the annual picnic sponsored by the H.J. Heinz Company in Leamington, Ontario. This firm, born in a little house in Sharpsburg, Pennsylvania, in 1869, expanded to London, England, in 1905 and in 1909 to Leamington, Ontario, the community that became known as "the tomato capital of Canada." The picnic tradition began in 1916 "as a way to help employees escape the rigours of the work-week." Held in August at Seacliff Park, it featured games, candy, ice cream, and a gigantic fireworks display that topped off the evening.

Are garden parties an extension of afternoon teas, picnics, or pleasure parties? We may never know, but whatever the origins, Canadian newspapers in the nineteenth century such as the *Canadian Illustrated News* of June 22, 1872, appear to approve of the trend:

> Tea in the arbour which used to be reckoned
> among the vulgarities of life has now got into
> society, and in this fine weather, when the
> sun is shining, and the sky is blue, and the
> grass is green it is much better to talk scan-
> dals in the garden than over tea-table indoors.

Maude C. Cooke, author of *Social Etiquette or Manners and Customs in Polite Society*, published in Toronto in 1896, confirms the popularity and ease of hosting a garden tea or a garden party: "Even the inexperienced hostess need only supply 'a green lawn, a few trees, a fine day and something to eat.'"

The guests, attired in their finest summer wardrobe, were welcomed on the lawn and invited to relax in easy chairs or hammocks. The food and beverages were laid out buffet-style on tables in the shade, under a marquee, or if a large gathering, on the dining room table indoors.

The hostess chose a menu that required little or no cutlery and might have included cold rolls, brown bread, butter, mixed sandwiches (salmon, cucumber, chicken, ham), biscuits, cheese, fancy cakes, fruit, iced tea, and lemonade. Small tables with fancy cloths and coloured napkins were scattered around the lawn, and the guests could repair to these or to their easy chairs to enjoy the dainties.

The celebrated garden parties at Buckingham Palace must have influenced many hostesses and party planners as two American guests can attest:

> Hundreds of elegant ladies in trailing gowns and picture hats, top-hatted gentlemen in formal attire, the royal bearing of Queen Mary, and the equally regal carriage of her six-year-old granddaughter — as though Elizabeth anticipated her future role.
>
> Never ending tables laden with traditional goodies — rock buns and mint sandwiches, Dundee cake and dark fruitcake, lemonade and orangeade. And, everyone sipped delicious chilled coffee topped with whipped cream from delicate demitasse cups.
>
> The party at Buckingham Palace was *the* model for garden parties all over the world![3]

Changes and improvements in transportation were to have an effect on garden parties in Canada as we glimpse the festive scene in a tiny community called Cedar Grove, Ontario, as well as the hazards of the Canadian weather:

> 1886: Monster Social — On Thursday evening last a Social was given by the members of the Presbyterian Church, Cedar Grove, on the beautiful grounds belonging to David Reesor, Esq., "Silver Spring Farm." The committee had made almost perfect arrangements to accommodate thousands. The ONTARIO and QUEBEC R.R. ran a special of eight cars from Toronto. The Massey Band, a concertina band, and the bagpipes were in attendance. Hundreds of ladened vehicles wended their way to the sylvan spot. The fifteen acre lawn, thickly and systematically studded with Norway spruce and other ornamental trees, and carpeted with luxurious soft grass closely shaven, was dotted all over with tables; the trees hung with Chinese lanterns were all prepared for simply lighting to render the scene almost too brilliant for earth, when down poured the rain in torrents.

Some 1,200 or 1,300 were on the grounds, and thousands more on the way or prepared to start for the sylvan scene. Those present filled and overran the palatial residence from the attic to the ground floor, even to the outer edges of the porticos. A few fortunate ones had partaken lunch off the well-laden tables before the rain fell. Mrs. Reesor (the hostess) was jolly throughout the affliction.[4]

With the passing years these social events were transformed into fundraisers, and one hostess was now assisted by the entire community to support a worthy cause.

Secret Societies:
Societies with Secrets or
Service Societies?

The men in our community really ruled the roost.
They lived the life of Riley.

— Kate Aitken

Canadian newspapers in the nineteenth and early twentieth centuries give us a surprising glimpse into the way communities, large and small, were organizing, serving, meeting, and celebrating. In 1898 the *Eastern Ontario Review* serving the village of Vankleek Hill and the surrounding district lists seven meetings, six for gentlemen, one for ladies. They include two Masonic Lodges, one to meet on the Tuesday on or before the full moon, another on the Wednesday on or before the full moon; the Loyal Orange Lodge to meet on the Friday on or before the full moon; the International Order of Foresters, the Patrons of Industry, the Sons of Temperance, and the Women's Christian Temperance Union.[1]

This pattern was repeated across Canada with fraternal, agricultural, industrial, religious, and historical service to the community as their objectives. For the most part membership in these organizations was limited to gentlemen, as the York Pioneer and Historical Society, founded in 1869, was open to gentlemen who resided in York when it became the City of Toronto in 1834. Membership was a dollar and stayed at that incredible sum until the early twentieth century. The temperance movement was to change those restrictions and statistics as women found themselves organizing in growing numbers to combat the abuse of alcohol in their communities.

Despite the proliferation of societies, one of the oldest and largest in early Canada was the Brotherhood of Freemasonry. Centuries ago, during the Middle Ages, stonemasons were much in demand as the construction of public buildings, abbeys, castles, cathedrals, churches, and even cottages demanded their skills. When they gathered to begin construction of a building, their first step was to build a small "lodge" where the workers could live, eat, and sleep while they worked on the larger building.

Since they lived together and worked together, shared knowledge and skills, and looked after one another in times of trouble, the masons formed bonds of fellowship and fraternity with fellow craftsmen and artisans. By the nineteenth century that was beginning to change with less demand for cathedral building, and the foundation was laid for a new membership of scholars, gentlemen, and all those interested in the ancient teachings of the society. In 1634 the lodge in Edinburgh is believed to be the first to accept and initiate a member who wasn't a working stonemason. We know that trend continued, for Robert Burns, the Scottish ploughman poet and tax collector, became a member of the St. David's (later St. James') Lodge in Tarbolton.

It is believed that the first Masonic lodge in Canada was formed among the members of the garrison at Halifax in 1749. There are also reports of lodges formed by members of the king's navy and the 8th Regiment of Foot, the King's Regiment, that served at Fort Niagara in 1773 and other locations in Upper Canada until 1785. A well-known member of the order was John Graves Simcoe, who commanded the First American Regiment, the original Queen's Rangers, from 1777 to 1781 during the American Revolution. When he was appointed lieutenant governor of the newly formed Upper Canada in 1791, he ensured the construction of the Masonic Lodge or Freemason's Hall, as it is generally known, in Newark (later Niagara-on-the-Lake). It was described as a two-storey building, with the upstairs rooms reserved for the meetings of the two lodges in the community, while the public rooms

downstairs were used by the Church of England for divine
worship, for dinner meetings of the Agricultural Society, for
the sitting of the court, as a ballroom, and as a First Nations
council room. Masons occasionally marched in processions,
often accompanied by a band, to one of the nearby taverns for
dinner to celebrate such special occasions as the Festival of St.
John the Evangelist on December 27.[2]

Another well-known member who also served the British
during the American Revolution was William Campbell, born
in Caithness, Scotland, in 1758. Campbell joined a Highland
Regiment at age twenty, was taken prisoner at Yorktown, and
eventually immigrated to Nova Scotia where he studied law.
He served as attorney general of Cape Breton and then was
appointed chief justice of Upper Canada in 1811. In his home
on Duke Street in York, Upper Canada, "Worshipful Brother
Campbell" held the preliminary meetings for St. Andrew's
Masonic Lodge.

Among the Irish settlers in Canada, the Orange Lodge was
very important since it united Irish Protestants in the frontier
society. It also engendered a good deal of publicity when the
eighteen-year-old Prince of Wales, Queen Victoria's eldest son,
visited in 1860. His tour began in St. John's, Newfoundland,
proceeded to the Atlantic colonies, and then to Canada East.
Members of the Orange Lodge in Canada West, particularly
in communities such as Kingston and Belleville, were dis-
tressed at the deference shown the Roman Catholic Church in

Canada East and demanded they be allowed to march in the parades when the prince reached their communities. To avoid a confrontation, the vessel the prince was travelling on didn't land at those communities, leaving the celebrants in tears and the celebrations in tatters.

For good or ill, parades were at the heart of the Orangeman's cause. Little Katie Scott (later Kate Aitken) growing up in the village of Beeton in the early twentieth century shares the excitement of a July12 parade:

> Our community boasted a strong Orange Order, which celebrated the Twelfth of July with pomp and circumstance. The Orange Lodge with its tightly battened windows lay midway down Centre Street. We had all heard terrifying stories of the goat that was kept locked up in the Orange Hall. We would steal down to the building, shinny up to the windowsills, then eye to a crack in the shutters, try to see what was hidden inside that locked enclosure; but we never found out.
>
> However, the night before the Twelfth of July the whole place was wide open. Members of the lodge came in to practice with fife and drum, and then lay out the order of the march. In our store Mother decorated dozens

of straw hats with orange-and-blue rosettes, then made up extra rosettes for the horses.

At eight o'clock the next morning visiting lodges began to arrive from Mount Ararat, from Cookstown, from Tottenham and from Schomberg. Each lodge had its own fife-and-drum band, its own Grand Master, its own beautifully decorated horses. But some lodge members had come unprepared, so Mother and Father were both busy handing out the fancied-up straw hats at twenty-five cents each, and horse rosettes for fifteen cents.

The route march, all on foot except for the horsemen, started at the Orange Hall with Isaac King, Grand Master of the Beeton Lodge, leading off. His white steed not only had the rosettes behind each ear but had orange and blue ribbons plaited all through the mane and tail. And Isaac King himself? There he was, mounted on his white horse, with his tall hat, his regalia complete with little gold apron, a picture for childish eyes. The Beeton Lodge was followed by all the visiting lodges. The procession marched down to the Grand Trunk Station, then turned back again up Centre Street. Wives of the Orangemen marched behind the lodges hanging onto their children, many of whom were dressed up to duplicate Dad's outfit.

Behind the regular procession came the hangers-on whose fathers weren't Orangemen, and amongst the crowd that lined the streets were good Roman Catholics from Adjala Township who had just happened to drop into Beeton on that particular day for a spot of shopping. There were no bad feelings, since a parade is always a parade, regardless of the objective.

After the march was completed, a picnic lunch was served at the fair grounds, complete with every farm delicacy that the wives of the Orangemen could provide. Centred at the speakers' table was a beautiful layer cake iced with orange-and-blue icing.[3]

From Katie we also learn one of the secrets of how many of the other organizations in her village managed their finances and their feasts:

Nearly everyone in the masculine world belonged to either the Orange Order or the Masonic Order. That meant at least one lodge night a week, which was as well established as the weekly church service. Most important annual event for the Masons was their annual supper with a guest speaker. That one night in the year the Masonic parlours were open to the women, who served the banquet. And these Masons shopped carefully. They went from one organization to the other — the Ladies' Aid, the W.M.S., the Pythian Sisters and the local hotels — trying to get a good meal at the lowest possible price. It took a lot of careful negotiating. The chairman of the local social committee would advise the Ladies' Aid: "The Pythian Sisters will give us a chicken dinner for fifty cents a plate." Whereas the Ladies' Aid would drop their price five cents a plate. So it usually ended up with a tip-top dinner with the best food the community could supply at thirty-five cents a head and no guaranteed attendance.

The lure of it all, of course, was the secrecy that surrounded the local lodge. Youngsters would volunteer to serve for nothing, hoping that they would get a glimpse of the mythical goat concealed in one of the back rooms.

> It was quite a sight to see the Masons in
> their regalia parading into the supper room
> and partaking liberally of the good things of
> this world.[4]

In the growing towns and cities of Canada, the societies were not always fortunate to have the support of women's organizations to "provide for them the good things of the world" at a modest cost. They often depended on caterers for their lavish feasts, such as the one enjoyed by the York Pioneers in the St. Lawrence Hall on Monday, April 17, 1871, to celebrate their second anniversary. The Bill of Fare included Mock Turtle or Oyster Soup, Salmon Trout with Anchovy Sauce, Codfish with Oyster Sauce, seven entrees followed by roasts of Sirloin of Beef with Horse Radish, Pork with Apple Sauce, Lamb with Mint Sauce, Saddle of Mutton with Currant Jelly, Chickens, and Turkey. A selection of boiled dishes included Corned Beef, Leg of Mutton with Caper Sauce, Hams, Tongues, and an array of vegetables. There were desserts to satisfy every taste from puddings to pastries to ices to cakes, with port and sherry, hot punch and beer, as beverages to complement this happy occasion.[5]

23

High Holy Days:
Rosh Hashanah and Yom Kippur

Who can say "I have purified my heart, I am free of sin?
There is no man on earth so righteous that he never sins!"
Cast away the evil you have done and get yourself
a new heart and a new spirit.

— Proverbs 20:9

osh Hashanah (New Year) and Yom Kippur (Day of Atonement) are the most important festivals of the Jewish religious year and are celebrated in either September or October. These are the times when Canadians of Jewish ancestry reflect on their life over the past year and ask God to forgive them for their sins. The days between Rosh

Hashanah and Yom Kippur are known as the Days of Awe, and during this period, Jews continue the process of reflection and self-examination.

This teaching has endured over the centuries and would have been known to those of Jewish ancestry arriving in colonial Canada. Among them was Myer Michaels, a Jewish fur trader, who received a crown grant in 1785 from Lieutenant Governor Patrick Sinclair for a lot at Fort Michilimackinac at the strait where Lake Huron joins Lakes Michigan and Superior. Myer Solomons, a Jew, was approved for a crown grant on Lot 25, Concession 2, in the Cornwall area in 1789, while John Lawe and John Levy Jacobs, of Jewish descent, received approval for town lots in Newark in 1794.[1] For those arrivals it must have been very difficult at times to observe their traditional religious and dietary restrictions.

George Benjamin and his young wife, Isabella, arrived in Toronto in 1834. George carried a small satchel, and inside among his few personal possessions was a small leather-bound book printed entirely in Hebrew. It was a prayer book for the holy day of Rosh Hashanah — the Jewish New Year — according to the Ashkenazic or Eastern European tradition.[2] George and Isabella made their home in Belleville where George became the founder, publisher, and editor of the town's *Intelligencer*, and served as reeve of Hungerford Township and warden of Hastings County. In 1856 he was elected a Member of Parliament for the Province of Canada. Benjamin was also elected and served as

Grand Master of the Orange Lodges of British North America with a membership of fifty thousand from 1846 to 1853. Meanwhile Isabella was raising a large family that eventually numbered fourteen children. In the fall of 1849 we learn that

> They were living much in the manner of their neighbours but privately maintained links with their religion. As always the Benjamins demonstrated a continuing concern about their children and their future chances of success. That autumn, Emmanuel Hyman (or Mannie as the family called him) was enrolled in Upper Canada College in Toronto and Esther Eliza (Ettie) was sent to boarding school in Montreal. On Friday, 24 September 1847, after the Jewish high holy days, the Benjamins arranged the baptism at St. Thomas' Church of their two oldest children, Mannie, born 1832, and Ettie, born 1836, just before the school season began.[3]

The holiday meal for Rosh Hashanah begins in the evening. *Challah*, the special bread for the festive meals, is dipped in honey to ensure a sweet new year. Fish, symbolizing fruitfulness and plenty, is also on the festive table, as seen in two favourite family fish recipes shared by Sondra Gotlieb:

GEFILTE FISH AS MOTHER MAKES IT
WITH LAKE WINNIPEG FISH

3 pounds, ground whitefish and pickerel
1 large onion, sliced finely
3 whole eggs
full tablespoon of salt
2 teaspoons ground black pepper
1 tablespoon sugar
1½ cups water
2 slices white bread, squeezed through
with water, and finely crumbled
additional sugar, salt, and pepper

Sauté onion until soft but not brown. Chop
even more finely and mix onion, fish, eggs,
water, bread, sugar, salt, pepper together
with an electric mixer. The fish-bread-eggs
mixture must be very fine. Pat into oval balls.

Slice up several carrots, onions, and celery
and put them in a large pot. Cover the vegetables with water and season with salt, pepper, and a tablespoon of sugar. Bring water to
a boil and drop fish balls carefully into sim-
mering water. Cook at a low temperature on

top of stove for 2½ hours.

Serve hot with vegetables and broth. Or serve cold with horseradish and sliced tomatoes.

AUNT DOLLY'S CHOPPED HERRING

2 large fat herring (these may be found in a barrel of brine at Jewish delicatessens)
2 large boiled eggs
1 green apple, chopped
1 thick slice of pumpernickel bread, soaked in a little vinegar
1 Spanish onion chopped

Soak herring in cold water overnight. Put cut-up fish, eggs, crumbled bread, apple through a food grinder. Season with salt, pepper, or sugar if needed. May be kept in refrigerator for several weeks. Eat with crackers or bread before the main course.[4]

Apples and honey are usually served at Rosh Hashanah to wish every one a sweet year. They can be combined and cooked to make wonderful desserts:

APPLESAUCE WITH HONEY

8 apples, peeled, halved, cored, preferably
Golden Delicious or Spy
½ cup honey
1 teaspoon cinnamon

Place apples in large, deep skillet. Add honey
and cinnamon. Bring to a boil and cook
until any liquid has evaporated, about 15 to
20 minutes. Purée or serve chunky. Makes
about 8 servings.[5]

HONEY CAKE

4 eggs
1 cup white sugar
1 pound honey (melted)
¾ cup oil
1 cup strong tea plus 1 teaspoon soda
2 teaspoons baking soda
1 teaspoon cinnamon
3¼ cups flour

Beat eggs; add sugar and honey and oil. Add flour and baking soda and cinnamon alternately with tea. Bake in greased tube pan 350 degrees 1 hour.[6]

Yom Kippur, the Day of Atonement, is the most solemn holy day of the Jewish religious year. The evening service that ushers in Yom Kippur is called Kol Nidre and is followed by four further ceremonies that begin the next morning and continue without interruption until sunset. This is a day of fasting and comes to a close with a long blast on the *shofar* and with the words "Hear, O Israel, the Lord our God, the Lord is One." Finally the promise "Next year in Jerusalem."

24

Labour Day

We labour soon, we labour late,
To feed the titled knave, man.
And a' the comfort we're to get
Is that ayont the grave, man.

— Robert Burns, "The Tree of Liberty"

For fishermen, fur traders, clergymen and women, explorers, and entrepreneurs who arrived on Canada's shores in the early days, an hourly, daily, weekly, or monthly salary was virtually unknown. Their goal was to survive and prosper, to overcome the challenges of climate and distance, and to learn the secrets of the endless forests and mysterious waterways they found here.

For the waves of settlers who followed them, the ownership of land, the clearing for a home, a garden, fields, and harvests, was of prime importance. Hard currency was in short supply, and barter, trade, and credit were commonplace in conducting business.

As communities grew, business and industry arrived and owners needed help to serve their customers or to complete their projects. Working for "room and board" was no longer an option. Those who needed help, or who were actually hiring, shared their opinions on the fluctuation in wages in the early nineteenth century in Upper Canada.

In 1815, Isaac Wilson, a settler on Yonge Street at York, wrote to his brother, Jonathon, that "The Government is carrying out a great many expensive undertakings at York such as building barracks storehouses wharfes and a house for the Governor. This makes labour very high and hands very hard to get. $1.50 per day being the common price with victuals and grog."[1] Two years later he again reports to his brother: "A great many mechanics have arrived at York from different parts of the States which reduced the price of labour considerably here. From $12.00 to $17.00 per month is the going rate now."[2]

In 1817, Daniel Sullivan, who was born in County Cork in Ireland and also took up residence in York, wrote home to his father that "tradesmen and labourers get very high wages; Carpenters and masons 10s; and labour is 5s per day, all the rest in proportion ..."[3]

It is also important to remember the role that mothers, wives, sisters, and daughters played in the ability of men to earn a salary, large or small:

> Men were required to work from sixty to seventy-two hours per week, and without wives to cook, sew, clean, bake and preserve, such a massive utilization of the male's energy would have been impossible ... when an employer hired a man, in effect he hired two people: the man to work on the job and the man's wife to keep the workman, physically and mentally, in working order. Although single men could "make do" by living in a boarding house, they were usually less desirable as employees.
>
> Finally, in an era when there was no medicare, workmen's compensation or old age pension, children were the only form of security available against illness, injury and old age. Parents raised children expecting to be supported by them at a later date. Without a wife and family, a working man could look forward to poverty and loneliness in his old age.[4]

By the second half of the nineteenth century in the growing towns, we find societies of workmen, joiners, carpenters, printers, and mechanics forming. News of these meetings were reported in the local papers, and some interesting responses emerged, as a master builder (no name given) writes in the *Patriot*, published in York on June 22, 1833:

> Observing an article in your paper of June 12, from a body of the Carpenters and Joiners of this town, who have formed themselves into a Society, under pretence of assisting any of their members who may sustain a loss by fire or robbery, or other accidental causes, I beg to inform the public, that this body have organized themselves for the sole purpose of suppressing their employers; by calling on them to comply with rules and regulations laid down by the body of Journeymen Carpenters; and to which the latter have all signed their names — sending a copy of the same to all their different employers in town: giving notice that after a certain date, they would not go to their work, unless their demands were complied with. The principle of these demands is; that five dollars must be paid them every week on account, and the

balance cleared up every month. Ridiculous demand! For under the present system in which money circulates, how is it possible that five dollars per week, can be collected every Saturday night, for 20 or 30 men, when money is scarce? and consequently long credit is expected.[5]

The war of words between workers and masters continued to escalate in Canada. However, it was in Australia in 1856 that stonemasons and building workers in Melbourne stopped work and marched to Parliament House to protest long hours. They were successful and are remembered as the first organized workers in the world to achieve an eight-hour day with no loss of pay. This was called the "eight-hour day movement," which advocated eight hours each for work, recreation, and rest![6]

It wasn't until 1872 that trade unions, which had been illegal until then, were given official recognition in Canada by the federal government. It was believed that a violent, city-wide strike of members of the Toronto Typographical Union brought this development about. Parades and picnics welcomed this news, and in 1886 the directors of the Industrial Exhibition of Toronto invited the city's labouring masses to the fair. They were offered free admission on condition that they march in procession with bands playing and banners flying. Apart from getting a free parade and swelling attendance figures, the exhibition directors were responding to what labour historians have called "The Great Upheaval."

In 1888 the Trades and Labour Congress petitioned the federal government for a national holiday. On July 23, 1894, an act was passed declaring the first Monday in September to be "Labour Day" and that indeed it would be celebrated as a national holiday. The parade continued to be an annual event at the renamed Canadian National Exhibition.[7]

September 3, 1894, saw a host of activities: Cheap-Labour Day Excursions by train; parades in many cities culminating in speeches; games and bountiful suppers in the parks; and bands to provide the music of celebration. There was a mood of optimism in the air as the nineteenth century drew to a close. Who would have guessed the economic downturn that was coming and the devastating effect it would have on the labour movement that had fought so hard for recognition, dignity, and equality?

The first years of the twentieth century heralded momentous events in Canada — millions of immigrants arriving from the United States, Great Britain, and eastern and southern Europe, with many of them headed for the territories between Manitoba and British Columbia; and the discovery of silver at Cobalt in 1903 and gold at Porcupine and Kirkland Lake, Ontario, a few years later. In addition there were new developments in transportation with the Wright Brothers achieving the first powered flight in 1903, and the

McLaughlin Motor Car Company being formed four years later to begin producing cars at Ewart McLaughlin's farm near Tyrone, Ontario. Refrigerated rail cars were developed in the late nineteenth century and had become increasingly dependable and sophisticated with each passing year. Ironically, at a time when Canadians should have been on the threshold of better days, improved living conditions, and new and imported foods on their tables, the Great Depression struck in 1929. Many Canadians found they were suddenly out of work, dependent on some level of government for food and clothing, commonly called "pogey," with far too many families realizing for the first time that popcorn went a long way toward filling an empty stomach.

Farm families had the best and the worst of the depression, for they had some degree of self-sufficiency with their gardens and fields of vegetables, grain for food for their livestock, as well as their skill and knowledge in the frugal husbanding of resources learned during years of crop failures. However, they now had to cope with the sudden return of family members who had left farms years before for the high-paying jobs in the industrialized towns and cities, and now, having lost those same jobs, were back on the farm to survive. As well, there were the "tramps," that steady stream of men knocking on doors, looking for a handout or a meal, and willing to do anything to pay for it. Tales were told of the marks the tramps put on a gatepost if they had been treated kindly and fed before being sent on their way, so that homeless men would know this was a refuge — for a few hours at least.

From the desperation of the Great Depression, many positive things finally emerged — credit unions, buying clubs, co-operative canneries, turkey pools, a revival of beef rings, the barter system, and many other enterprises that helped thousands of Canadians to earn their own living through their own efforts. In Canadian kitchens, cooks learned how to make something of nothing, or next to nothing. Recipes for Economy Cake, Save All Pie, and Economical Chicken Salad that used only a cup of chicken to feed a family of ten were used whenever a family was fortunate enough to have the ingredients to make them. For those families still eating three meals a day, they could expect to have porridge for breakfast, bread fried in lard or drippings for dinner at noon, and maca-roni for supper, all washed down with strong, hot tea.

Enterprising and innovative cooks developed new recipes for macaroni and cheese, macaroni and tomatoes, fried bread, bread pudding, casseroles of bread stuffing, and every con-ceivable form of baked and steamed bread, biscuits, dump-lings, and puddings. Using up leftovers by combining them with other leftovers and perhaps adding a new ingredient was honed to a fine art. "Make it do, make it over, use it up" became every Canadian's motto.

POOR MAN'S CAKE

2 cups brown sugar
½ pound lard
1 scant teaspoon salt
2 teaspoons cinnamon
1 teaspoon cloves
1 teaspoon nutmeg
1 teaspoon soda
½ cup currants (rinsed in hot water)
1½ cups water
3½ cups flour

Mix all ingredients in a large bowl. Grease an 8-inch-square pan and bake 50 minutes in a moderate oven of 350 degrees. This can be served plain, with icing, or with a sauce.

Sauce for Poor Man's Cake

Melt 1 tablespoon butter or margarine in a saucepan and remove from heat. Add 2 table-spoons flour and ¼ cup of brown sugar. Stir well and return to heat, slowly adding water (about 1 ½ cups), stirring all the while. When well blended and thick, remove and serve.

HARD TIMES PUDDING

Half a pint of molasses
Half a pint of water
Two teaspoons of soda
One teaspoon of salt

Thicken with flour enough to make a batter about like that for a cup cake. Put this in a pudding-bag; allow room to rise. It would be safe to have the pudding-bag about half full of the batter. Let this boil for three hours.

Sauce to serve with this is made thus: Mix two teaspoonfuls of either white or brown sugar with a lump of butter the size of a butternut; a little salt and one large spoonful of flour should be mixed with the butter and sugar. When free from lumps pour boiling water slowly over it, stirring all the time. Let it boil up once or twice to make it the desired thickness.

MOCK CHERRY PIE

1 cup cranberries (cut in halves)
1 cup sugar

1 teaspoon vanilla
1 tablespoon flour dissolved in
½ cup water
1 egg
Mix well all ingredients and bake between
two crusts of your favourite pastry.

LEFT OVER MUFFINS

Remember that muffins left over from one
meal can be pulled, not cut, apart, and toasted
for the next meal.

"Make it do, make it over, use it up!"

25

Let Us Give Thanks

Come, ye thankful people, come,
Raise the song of harvest home!
All is safely gathered in,
Ere the winter storms begin.

— Henry Alford, "Come, Ye Thankful People, Come"

Celebrating and giving thanks for a good harvest are ancient traditions steeped in superstitions, folklore, and legends. When the harvest moon appeared in northern skies, the ancients knew that the warm weather was leaving and the storms of winter would soon be upon them. From medieval times the traditions of harvesting, storing, and feasting with family and friends emerged. The last of the crop, whatever it might be, was often harvested with great ceremony and then decorated with ribbons of cloth to symbolize a human figure. This was often called the Harvest Queen or Kern Doll and was kept in a place of honour until it was time to plant the crops the following year.

It is from the medieval period that the ancient celebration of Harvest Festival or "Harvest Home" arose among the farmers of rural England. The tradition of a thanksgiving celebration in Canada is as old as the country itself, for there were many thanksgivings before an official day was chosen.

For centuries before the arrival of newcomers on Canadian shores, the First Nations were giving thanks to their Sacred Mother for the harvest they were gathering and preparing to store for the long winter ahead. They had been celebrating the green corn harvest for centuries. The Iroquois ceremony lasted for three days and honoured the Three Sisters — corn (their Sacred Mother), beans, and squash. The Harvest Moon guided the First Nations to travel to the cranberry (crane berry) bogs to gather the small sour red berries so important to them as a medicine and to be used in foods and beverages. They enjoyed them both raw and cooked, sometimes sweetened with maple syrup or maple sugar.

Wild rice played an important part in the social, economic, and ceremonial life of the First Nations, particularly the Algonquin, Ojibwa, and Northern Cree, as they moved to their camps near the shallow waters of the northern Great Lakes and the lakes in Manitoba and Saskatchewan. At that time of year they held Wild Rice Festivals as they harvested this precious "good berry" so important to their survival over the winter. Harvested by the women and processed by the men, wild rice was also an important barter item on their trading routes that stretched from the Gulf of Mexico to James Bay. The First Nations also enjoyed a feast when the hunt was successful, the fish ran in abundance, or they found a windfall of fruit or other natural foods.

The explorers, entrepreneurs, fishermen, and adventurers who were probing the northern coasts of North America in the sixteenth century would have been aware of thanksgiving prayers and services in their homelands. Many of them may have also been aware of the traditions of the First Nations as they met, bartered, and traded.

In the summer of 1578, Martin Frobisher was attempting for the third time to find the Northwest Passage to the riches of Cathay. Separated from the rest of the fleet and lost in a storm in July, Frobisher and his crew despaired for their lives. By August the vessels reunited on the Countess of Warwick Island, and the Reverend Robert Woolfall who was aboard the *Nancy* led a service of thanksgiving:

> Here euery man greatly rejoiced of their happie
> meeting, and welcommed one another, after

the Sea manner with their great Ordinance, and when each partie had ripped vp their sundry fortunes and perils past, they highly praysed God, and altogiher vpon their knees gaue him due, humble and heartie thankes, and Maister Wolfall a learned man, appointed by her Maiesties Councell to be their Minister and Preacheer made vnto them a godly sermon, exhorting them specially to be thankfull to God for their strange and miraculous deliuerancce in those dangerous places, and putting them in mind of vncertintie of mans life, willed them to make themelues alwayes readie as resolute men to enjoy and accept thankfully what soeuer aduenture his diuine Prouidece should appoint.[1]

Frobisher and his men then tucked into plates of salt beef, sea biscuits, and peas. These would have been standard rations in the sixteenth century on British ships, and the sailors had eaten them many times before, but not with such enthusiasm as they did when giving thanks for their survival.

This was the beginning of many informal thanksgiving services and meals, including 1710 in Port Royal when Nova Scotia passed into English hands; 1763 in Halifax when the Treaty of Paris ended the Seven Years' War; 1799 in Lower

Canada when thanksgiving was celebrated; and 1816 in Upper Canada when it gave thanks for the end of the war between Great Britain and France.

On at least two occasions the royal family decreed the celebration. In 1856, Queen Victoria proclaimed July 4 a day of thanksgiving in recognition of Britain's victory in the Crimean War, and April 15, 1872, officially marked the recovery of the Prince of Wales (later King Edward VII) from a very serious illness.

The Province of Canada created the nation's first Thanksgiving Day in 1859 with a declaration asking all Canadians to spend the holiday in "public and solemn" recognition of God's mercies. It appears that clergymen, politicians, and merchants were all struggling to control the day. A day of worship? A day of fellowship and feasting with family and friends? A trip by train at "special rates"? Or shopping for the "Thanksgiving goods" advertised by local merchants?

Finally, on October 9, 1879, the Marquis of Lorne, then governor general, proclaimed a statutory holiday on November 6 and "a day of General Thanksgiving to Almighty God for the bountiful harvest with which Canada had been blessed."

For several years thanksgiving celebrations in Canada moved through October, November, and December and were combined for a while with Remembrance Day. At another time the feast was celebrated American-style in late November. None of these were satisfactory, and finally in 1957 Parliament passed legislation making Thanksgiving Day an annual holiday celebrated on the second Monday of October.

Late summer and early fall was the period when farmers' markets became particularly popular. First Nations had long bartered and traded ingredients and food; the newcomers brought the market tradition with them, and formal market days were established in many communities by the eighteenth century. Some specialized in meat, fish, fowl, or game, but most showcased and sold the harvest from local gardens and farms.

The weeks leading up to Thanksgiving, whenever it was celebrated, would have been the busiest of the year, particularly for farm families. With the short growing season in many parts of Canada, not a minute was to be lost in harvesting, preserving, and storing the harvest for the long months ahead.

Housewives had been picking, drying, or preserving (with honey, maple syrup, or sugar) wild and cultivated fruit as it ripened all summer long, including strawberries, raspberries, gooseberries, plums, peaches, cherries, chokecherries, red and black currants, gooseberries, cranberries (both high and low bush), blueberries, pinchberries, apples, pears, crabapples, and more!

Root vegetables from the garden could be packed in sawdust or sand and stored in a cool, dry place. Potatoes, carrots, turnips, onions, and parsnips were the mainstay of many tables for months to come. Carrots and potatoes were finely chopped when they were needed to use in puddings, cookies, and pancakes, as well.

Not only were the men of the farm speeding to harvest the crops in the fields, thresh the grain, and store the straw and precious seeds in the barn, but they also had to make decisions about their animals. How many could they house over the winter and how many needed to be slaughtered? The butchering of animals and preparing the meat for storage was not only hard work but had to be carried out quickly. Often a bee was held, with several farmers doing the butchering. In the kitchen the women rendered the fat, cleansing the intestines in readiness for sausage casings and making head cheese. This was the time to make Blood Pudding, also called Blood Sausage or Black Pudding. This centuries' old dish includes fat, onions, herbs, oatmeal, and liver in many variations. Nothing was wasted!

To provide some zest to the meat and vegetables destined for their tables, this was also the period to preserve pickles and relishes. Depending on taste and yield, these could include Corn, Cucumber, or Rhubarb Relish; Mustard, Nine Day, Dill, and Bread and Butter Pickles; Pickled Beets or Onions; Tomato Chili Sauce; and Green Tomato Mincemeat.

If we could return to the early twentieth century and travel across Canada, what would we find on the harvest or Thanksgiving tables of our ancestors? Here are some suggestions:

Newfoundland
Pea Soup, Flipper Pie, Moose Steak, Beets, Plain Boiled Pudding with Screech Sauce or Partridgeberry Sauce, or Partridgeberry Tart (Pie)

Prince Edward Island
Beef Barley Vegetable Soup, Roast Pork with Apples, Potato Pancakes, Rutabagas, Carrot Pudding with Rum Runner Sauce

Nova Scotia
Clam Chowder, Roast Turkey with Oyster Stuffing, Maple Syrup Squash, Cranberry Relish, Mincemeat or Apple Pie

New Brunswick
Cod Cheeks and Tongues, Chicken Stew with Dumplings, Turnip Potato Hash, Cranberry Pie or Sweet Apple Pastries with Sugar Sauce

Quebec
Petit Caribou, Pickled Pigs Feet or Roast Pork or Meatball Stew, Pickled Beets, Apple Dumplings or Maple Syrup Pie, Red Wine, Black Currant Liqueur

Ontario

Sweet Apple Cider, Roast Turkey with Bread Stuffing, Mashed Potatoes with Gravy, Mashed Turnips, Green Beans, Cranberry Sauce, Pumpkin Pie with Whipped Cream

Manitoba

Bannock or Corn Fritters, Partridge with Wild Rice Stuffing, Baked Acorn Squash, Scalloped Potatoes, Carrot Pudding with Brandy Butter, Cream Puffs in Chocolate Sauce

Saskatchewan

Roast Turkey, Roast Mallard Duck with Onion Dressing, Wild Rice Casserole, Parsnips, Turnips, Potatoes, Saskatoon Berry Pie or Apple Pie

Alberta

Alberta Onion Soup, Chicken or Sweet and Sour Ribs or Beef, Saddle Bag Spuds, Rum Trader Beans, Baked Lemon Pudding

British Columbia

Bannock with Wild Rose Jelly, Teriyaki Chicken or Arctic Char Steaks, Honey

Carrots, Fried Green Tomatoes, Apple Blueberry Crisp[2]

This season, and this day, was truly one of thanksgiving
for our ancestors. They had worked long and hard to prepare
for the winter that was fast approaching. As they sat down
together with family and friends, they were certainly giving
thanks "to Almighty God for the bountiful harvest with which
Canada has been blessed." As Lydia Maria Child's 1844 poem
and song "A Boy's Thanksgiving Day" says:

> Over the river, and through the wood,
> Trot fast my dappled grey!
> Spring over the ground like a hunting-
> hound!
> For 'tis Thanksgiving Day!
> ...
> Over the river, and through the wood,
> Now Grandmother's cap I spy!
> Hurrah for the fun! Is the pudding done?
> Hurrah for the pumpkin pie!

26

All Hallows' Eve, All Saints' Day, and All Souls' Day

'Tis now the very witching time of night,
When churchyards yawn and hell itself breathes out
Contagion to this world ...

— William Shakespeare, *Hamlet*

From ghoulies and ghosties
And long-leggety beasties
And things that go bump in the night,
Good Lord, deliver us!

— Scottish Saying

The end of October and the beginning of November was, for the ancients, a time of feasting, fasting, and remembrance of their loved ones. Over the centuries a host of folk customs, traditions, beliefs, and superstitions have been combined and celebrated during a three-day period.

The origins of All Hallows' Eve, Halloween, may go back to the ancient Romans, who at that time of year held a feast in honour of Pomona, the goddess of tree fruit such as apples, pears, and cherries. For the Celts who dominated the British Isles, parts of northern Europe, and France thousands of years ago, their calendar had only two seasons: winter, which began on November 1 and ended on April 30; and summer, which started on May 1 and finished on October 31. The Celts believed that October 31 was the day the old year died, and for their priests, the Druids, this day and night was called Samhain, or the Festival of Summer's End, in honour of their chief god, the Lord of the Dead. The Druids led their people in the ceremonies, offerings, and sacrifices that were all part of the celebration. The last of the fruit and grain was harvested and stored safely away, the herds of sheep, goats, and cattle were sheltered in the barns, and all preparations were made for the long, dark, cold months ahead.

This was the time to set fires on the hillsides to strengthen the weakening sun and to welcome the spirits of their ancestors as they believed the veil between the physical world and the Otherworld was very thin on this night, and thus spirits and mortals could pass easily between the two. Special foods were prepared and set out for the ancestors, and as everyone feasted they told stories about their ancestors and their families. Black cats had a place in these stories as the Druids believed they had once been human beings who were changed into cats for their misdeeds.

As Christianity began to emerge as a dominant force in Europe, there was an attempt to adapt the ancient pagan festivals to the new Christian celebrations and calendar. In 731 A.D., Pope Gregory III designated November 1 as All Hallows' Day or All Saints' Day to commemorate all the lesser saints who couldn't have a feast especially set aside for them, as well as for all holy men, women, and martyrs whose record of good deeds hadn't survived. The next day, November 2, became known as All Souls' Day when prayers would be offered for all the deceased whose souls were in a special waiting place called Purgatory.

All Hallows' Eve was once observed as a fast day and later as a meatless day with pancakes or Callcannon (Kall Cannon, Call Cannon), a combination of potatoes and other vegetables cooked and mashed.

There were many traditions and superstitions to foretell the future, since everyone wanted to know what the New Year had in store for them. Tokens were hidden in serving dishes, such as thimbles, rings, wheels, coins, or toys, each with their own meaning. Hallowmas or Sallain Bannock (a very salty cake) was eaten by single maidens just before bed so they would dream about their future husbands.

November 2, All Souls' Day, became the day when the French placed artificial flowers on the graves of their ancestors, and many cultural groups put offerings of the favourite foods of departed family members on their last resting place.

There are many records of housewives making Sau'mas Loaves "with currants in the centre" that were very similar to the Hot Cross Buns we associate with Good Friday and the celebration of Easter Sunday. In Wales, bakers made these small loaves and gave them to their customers, who kept them in their homes to bring good luck. Soul Cakes or Souly Cakes are still baked in Wales in the form of yeast buns, brown, spiced, and shining, with a round head, currants for eyes, a semicircular smile, two arms represented by cuts in the body, and two legs. These are, of course, great favourites with children, who in some communities go door to door chanting:

> A soul-cake, a soul-cake
> Please good mistress a soul-cake;
> One for Peter and one for Paul
> And one for the Lord who made us all
> An apple, a pear, a plum or a cherry,
> Any good thing will make us merry.[1]

In addition to lighting fires and preparing food for the return of departed loved ones, All Hallows' Eve began to develop new traditions as various cultural groups celebrated the festival. The Irish are credited with the jack-o'-lantern, made from carving a turnip or a potato to look like a human head so that a candle could be placed inside and it could be carried around as a charm against evil. The lantern was named after a tailor called Jack who angered both God and the Devil and wasn't allowed to enter either Heaven or Hell but was forced to wander the planet until Judgment Day carrying his lighted turnip to find his way.

The Scots contributed many traditions to the celebration and also focused on food, beverages, and forecasting the future. Bobbing for Apples was a favourite that was practised by courting couples. Each apple was given the name of a desired mate. If the bobber succeeded in biting the apple on the first try, then love would thrive. If the apple was caught on the second bite, love would exist only briefly. Success on the third chance meant hate, not love. Apple Parings gave everyone an opportunity to peel an apple using a small knife. The long spiral of the apple peeling was thrown over the left shoulder, and when it landed, it would resemble the first letter of a sweetheart's name. Nutcracker involved a couple placing two nuts in a fire and watching what happened to them. If the heated nuts burst their shells and crackled loudly, that was a sign of true love; however, if they just burned, the love would soon perish. Crowdie was a particularly delicious Halloween food. A large bowl was prepared containing whipped cream, applesauce, and oatmeal. Objects such as rings, marbles, and coins that were carefully scrubbed were dropped into the bowl. Guests were given spoons to taste the Crowdie carefully, but not to swallow the "fortune." Finding the ring meant a marriage, the coin wealth, the marble a single life. Finding nothing signified a life of sweet uncertainty.

The Acadians in Cape Breton served La Soupe au Chou (Cabbage Soup) on Halloween, since they considered it a meatless day and fasted on the Vigil of All Saints' Day. The Irish, Scots, and Germans who settled in Nova Scotia all made and enjoyed the traditional Kohl Cannon, with the coins, rings, buttons, and matches (all were wrapped) dropped into it, heralding their future prospects.

In Newfoundland the first meal of Call Cannon for the year was cooked on the evening of October 31. By that time most of the vegetables were harvested and put in the root cellar for winter keeping. On this occasion neighbours would share and exchange the various vegetables from their gardens with one another, and the night of the meal was always called Call Cannon Night.[2]

Forach, a rich dessert served in Scottish homes, also travelled to Nova Scotia. A combination of fine oatmeal, sugar, and whipping cream, with a wedding ring dropped into it, to be found by a lucky young maiden who believed she was the next to be married. Pumpkins were so plentiful in Canada that they were soon substituted for the turnips and potatoes when carving a jack-o'-lantern for a trip in the darkness on Halloween.

In the Red River Settlement in today's Manitoba, Halloween was celebrated in the 1860s and 1870s by children wearing masks, dressing in costume, and playing pranks. Canadian newspapers carried stories of young people in Prince Edward Island carrying lighted cattails that had been soaked in kerosene for several days as they went around in old clothes looking for treats. Tricks were played on those who didn't give a treat. One of the most popular tricks was to remove and hide the gates that hung at the entrance to farm properties.

In Toronto an Anti-Treating Society was formed, and in 1876 the *Daily Globe* carried an article describing a free concert held the night before in a schoolhouse where the minister of All Saints' Church gave readings, the church choir sang, and piano solos were given to keep trick-or-treaters off the streets. In 1890 in Halifax at the Queen's Hotel, apple bobbing was on the program. However, it was the bellboys who bobbed, not the guests. Those lads were looking for coins, not their true loves!

As the years passed, the celebration of All Hallows' Eve or Halloween moved farther from its origins, while for those Canadians who celebrate All Saints' Day and All Souls' Day, the traditions have continued of attending worship on the first day and remembering relatives, ancestors, and friends, and later a feast of the finest and best-loved foods in the family.

On All Souls' Day the tradition of visiting a place of worship and then of visiting the graves of loved ones continues. For some families it is a simple, prayerful watch, while for others it is a hamper of favourite foods, including Soul

Cakes, one for each of the departed, and one for all those honouring them.

In Canada, Halloween continues to be celebrated by children and young people going door to door dressed in costumes, wearing masks, and occasionally carrying jack-o'-lanterns. As they knock on the door and call "Trick or treat," most people happily respond by giving them candies, cookies, or fruit.

You may not be a member of an Anti-Treating Society, but you still may want to keep your family at home for Halloween. Here are some simple suggestions from the early twentieth century:

> For the centrepiece for your table start with the bare branch of a tree anchored in a firm base. Trim it with tiny black cats and witches' hats. For your place cards use black half masks, names lettered on them in white. Serve scoops of orange sherbet with gumdrops stuck in them to form features of jack-o'-lanterns and pumpkin-shaped cookies.

Need something hearty? Here is a simple menu:

Hobgoblin Hamburgers
Jack-o'-Lantern Salad

Individual Pumpkin Pies
(with small yellow cheese pumpkins) ·
Apple Juice or Apple Cider

For Hobgoblin Hamburgers, make a face on top of each split round hamburger roll as follows: with toothpicks arrange sliced pimento-stuffed olives for eyes; a whole pitted olive for a nose. For the mouth, make ghoulish grins by cutting or tearing the surface of the roll. Insert your favourite hot hamburger patty in each roll and prepare to serve. Warn guests about the toothpicks! Serve fruit salad in hollowed-out orange shells, or fresh or canned peach halves.[3]

27

Remember,
Remember the Fifth of November

Remember, remember the Fifth of November,
The Gunpowder Treason and Plot,
I see no reason
Why the Gunpowder Treason
Should ever be forgot.

— Traditional Rhyme

"The Canadians are thoroughly a people for amusement, and enjoy all kinds of recreation exceedingly. They follow out the customs of the English to a great extent, and participate freely in the games so loved in the old country,"[1] observed visitors to Upper Canada in the middle of the nineteenth century. Surely, it isn't a coincidence then that it is in Newfoundland, Britain's oldest colony, that Guy Fawkes Night or Bonfire Night is still celebrated.

To learn its origins we return to England under the reign of King James I. James had already been king of Scotland for many years, so now called himself James VI and I, and as a Protestant inherited the long struggle to take power away from the Roman Catholic Church and its members and place it firmly with the established religion — the Church of England. The Catholics were angry, and the boldest of their leaders came up with a plan to kill James and take control of the country. They knew that when the king opened Parliament he usually made a speech in the House of Lords, surrounded by the royal princes and his leading ministers, with the leaders of the House of Commons in attendance, as well.

> The scheme was to blow up all of these at once by storing barrels of gunpowder in the basement of the House of Lords, packing bars of iron in tightly on top, and firing this giant bomb when the king made his speech. All the Protestant leaders of the country thus being killed at once, the Catholics were to seize control of the government, bring up young princess Elizabeth as a Catholic and make her queen.

The man chosen to bring about the actual explosion was Guy Fawkes, a brave officer who had much experience in planning mines in warfare. He was to light a slow "match" which would take a quarter of an hour to reach and fire the gunpowder. A boat was to wait by the Westminster steps to take him at once back on board a ship leaving for Flanders.... A mysterious warning reached the king. Men came down into the basement, asked Guy Fawkes a question or two about the store of firewood he was supposed to be keeping there, and went away. That night, November 4th, 1605, he was arrested after a struggle.... The other conspirators were soon crushed and most shot down after a long chase.... At that time it was the custom to celebrate good news by lighting bonfires in the streets. When the news of the plot and its failure got about, crowds gathered and celebrated. Fireworks had recently been improved, and many a one was set off on that November 5th.[2]

Bonfire Night is still celebrated in Great Britain, and many Canadians have fond memories of their childhood preparations. During the day, old clothes were stuffed with straw to form an effigy of Guy Fawkes, which was then loaded into an old baby carriage, cart, or homemade wagon. A group of children banded together and walked through the neighbourhood, chanting and calling for "A penny for the guy, a penny for the guy!" Then it was off to the shops to buy fireworks for the evening when the bonfire would be lighted in a green space or local park. The favourite of all fireworks was the Catherine Wheel, named for St. Catherine, who was martyred on a wheel. Scrap wood was gathered and piled in the park ready for the bonfire to be ignited as soon as supper was finished. If families had a large community garden, they might have their bonfire and fireworks there.[3]

On at least one occasion the drama of the evening was intense. A family that lived near a local park always had its piano lifted out of the house to be used for the singalong that was part of the festivities. Unfortunately, it began to rain, and as the children were holding precious fireworks in their hands, they decided to store them in the piano to keep them dry. Shortly afterward, one of the adults lifted the lid of the piano to light one of the fireworks and accidentally dropped his match into the piano. The remaining fireworks and the piano exploded and brightened the night sky for miles. This event became part of the community's folklore for years.[4]

Just as those stories have survived and crossed the ocean, so have the memories and tales of Guy Fawkes Night or Bonfire Night continued in Newfoundland and Labrador. Gail Alice Collins, who grew up in Newfoundland, tells us:

Planning began in early fall. Bonfire Night required skill, strategy and hard work. First we chose our co-conspirators. It was important to get along. From early October until Nov. 5 you'd be spending every available hour together.

Next we chose our location.... In my garden, there was prime space near the back, where we could see and be seen.... We scrounged papers, old chairs, broken pickets, lobster traps ... we'd beg aunts, uncles and cousins to save their old catalogues and anything else for our fire.

At Halloween, we paused for costumes and trick-or-treating: a little breather before the big push.

Just at dark, on the great night, we'd gather around our creation: a towering mound of boughs, papers and boards. We were proud as if we'd built the pyramids. Our parents were invited too. We wanted them to appreciate what we had wrought. And although we had built the fire, only an adult was permitted to light it ... the flames whooshed throughout the whole pile into the air ... as we cheered. From our vantage point we could see in all directions. The hills of the harbour were dotted with flames: a ring of fire beating back the darkness of the night.

Our faces hot, our backs to the cold night, we toasted marshmallows and wieners. Later we'd poke around in the embers, routing out the roasted potatoes; tearing off their blackened jackets to eat the fragrant meat within.[5]

As well as roasting potatoes, salt fish was also a favourite to heat on a long stick over the fire. It sounds as if some tricking (similar to Halloween) went on in some communities on this night, as stories are told of young lads in Newfoundland setting outbuildings alight along with the bonfires.[6]

On Bell Island in Newfoundland the competition for the biggest and longest-lasting bonfire was intense. The search for old tires, carrying away small buildings (such as outhouses), and raiding other group's piles of wood were all part of the excitement. As a result, some fires would burn for a week![7]

28

Lest We Forget

In Flanders fields the poppies blow
Between the crosses, row on row ...

— Lieutenant-Colonel John McCrae,
"In Flanders Fields"

The eleventh hour of the eleventh day of the eleventh month, November 11, 1918, marked the end of the First World War. Canada, despite its short history, had already been involved in several wars, and this was the war to end all wars. Sixty thousand Canadian soldiers had given their lives in the conflict and were buried in graveyards in Europe by the time armistice documents were signed. Known as Armistice Day for many years, it has been forever remembered because of the poem of tribute written by a young Guelph, Ontario, doctor, Major (later Lieutenant-Colonel) John McCrae, at a medical aid station at Essex Farm near Ypres in 1915.

In Flanders fields the poppies blow
Between the crosses, row on row,
That mark our place; and in the sky
The larks, still bravely singing, fly
Scarce heard among the guns below.

We are the Dead. Short days ago
We lived, felt dawn, saw sunset glow,
Loved and were loved, and now we lie
In Flanders fields.

Take up our quarrel with the foe:
To you from failing hands we throw
The torch, be yours to hold it high.
If ye break faith with us who die
We shall not sleep, though poppies grow
In Flanders fields.

"In Flanders Fields" was published in *Punch* in December 1915 and inspired the use of the poppy as an enduring symbol of remembrance. McCrae died and was buried at Wimereux, France, in January 1918.

In 1931 the Canadian Parliament changed the name of this special day to Remembrance Day and declared it a legal holiday. As time passed, it has become the day to remember all Canadians who have served and given their lives in the many conflicts Canada has been involved in. Parades, church services, the laying of wreaths and fresh flowers in public parks, monuments, cenotaphs, tombs, and cemeteries, special dinners and banquets, have all become part of the memories. It is also a time to wear poppies, immortalized by McCrae's poem.

Long before the arrival of newcomers on Canada's shores, the First Nations were honouring their dead in a number of different ways. Samuel de Champlain noted that in 1608, following the death of a chief, the Natives would hold a feast three times a year and sing and dance on the grave. A few years later he described a cemetery on the Ottawa River with tombs like shrines embellished with articles the deceased might need in the spirit world. For example, if the departed were a woman or a girl, a kettle, an earthen pot, a wooden spoon, a paddle, or other food-related artifact might be depicted.

On September 28, 1635, Father LeJeune provided an account of a Feast for the Dead that he and Father Buteux attended, and noted that the Natives gave the departed the best part of the banquet. The Anishnawbe First Nation shares its knowledge of the continuing ceremony with us:

The feast for honouring and feeding the dead

is held in the fall, and in some communities, also in the winter. A sacred fire burns for four days and a food offering is made for the person each day before sundown. A ceremony is held before the feast where it is said you eat with your relative for the last time.

The feast begins with prayers and an offering of tobacco. The people and directions are acknowledged and the spirits are told what is being done. The food is set out on the table.

The foods prepared include those that the relatives and ancestors liked when they lived here. This might be wild meat, corn, squash, and berries. Other foods and teas, such as cedar tea, raspberry tea, and red willow tea, are added to these four basic foods. Salmon, bannock and wild rice are other foods included in the feasts. The smudge bowl is taken around and the food and people are smudged.

Gifts of cloth and leather are also given with the foods and tobacco offerings for the spirits.

Out of respect, the younger ones make up a plate of food for the Elders. By doing this, the younger ones learn about taking care of another human being. The Elders are the

first to be served and then the other participants follow a specific order. As the feasters
make up their plate of food from the dishes
laid out on the table, they put a spoonful of
food for their relatives and ancestors into a
pot set out for this purpose. At the end of the
feast this pot is taken outside and the food is
set on the ground for the spirits. Any food
remaining on the table at the end of the feast
is taken out and put on the ground or burned
when the sun comes up in the morning. It is
said that during the night, many spirits come
from every direction to share in the feast. The
spirits of relatives and ancestors bring other
spirits who haven't been remembered and
they share the food with them.[1]

Many newcomers believed that when death occurred they
should cover their beehives with black drapery, hum a mourn-
ful tune, and announce the name of the deceased so that the
heavenly messengers would take the news to heaven. Meanwhile
neighbours and friends prepared ready-made dishes of food
and delivered them to the mourning family, many of whom
had travelled long distances for the funeral service, whether at
home, at a place of worship, or at the graveside. This was followed by a hearty meal washed down with strong lashings of tea

or a plentiful supply of spirits depending on the family's beliefs and wishes.

From Nova Scotia we learn that "A generous table was laid with barley bread and cheese, loaf cake and always a funeral cake, which was a plain cake flavoured with cinnamon. A funeral rated a good supply of liquor."[2]

We find cinnamon in many recipes for funeral foods. Cinnamon was once among the most precious of spices, five times more valuable than silver, according to Pliny the Elder in the first century A.D., but as it decreased in value it became the most popular of all spices. The culinary realm that holds it most dear is that of sweets — cakes, desserts, liqueurs.[3]

Hemmingford Village in Quebec celebrated the hundredth anniversary of its incorporation by publishing *Old Hemmingford Recipes*, including early settlers' memories and favourite foods. What follows is an early settler's recipe that would have been served after a funeral:

FUNERAL PIE

1 unbaked pie shell
2 cups sour cream
½ cup raisins
1½ cups brown sugar (packed)
¼ teaspoon salt
2 eggs, beaten

2 tablespoons cornstarch
1 tablespoon lemon juice
¼ teaspoon nutmeg
¼ teaspoon cinnamon
pinch cloves[4]

Greek settlers coming to Manitoba at the end of the nineteenth century brought with them the tradition of preparing Kolliva (also Kolyva) for a mourning service held forty days after the passing of a loved one. This dish contains boiled wheat, symbolizing everlasting life, raisins for sweetness, chopped nuts, cinnamon, and crushed zwieback. It is covered with a thick layer of sugar, and a depression in the form of a cross is made on the top and then filled with silver candy.[5]

New arrivals from China arriving in Canada in the mid-nineteenth century brought with them the tradition of Quing Ming, a spring celebration to honour the deceased. A family would travel to the cemetery, graves would be cleaned, fresh flowers planted, spirits poured over the graves, and a picnic lunch enjoyed right there with their ancestors.[6]

Many communities in Canada, regardless of their cultural traditions, hold memorial services at their local cemeteries to remember and honour those who have gone before. Fresh flowers, music, and words of comfort are all part of the ceremony. At the conclusion everyone is invited to take part in a time of good food and fellowship and of course the sharing of memories.

29

La Tire Ste-Catherine

Once in a young lifetime one should be allowed to have
as much sweetness as one can possibly want and hold.

— Judith Olney

For many French Canadians, St. Catherine's Day is linked to love, marriage, sweet treats, and the fun of taffy pulling!

Catherine lived in Alexandria and was martyred on November 25, 307 A.D. Legend tells us she was ordered to be tortured on a spiked wheel by Roman Emperor Maximus, and when the wheel broke at her touch, she was beheaded.

This wheel is still remembered as a popular spinning type of fireworks called a Catherine Wheel. It is very popular with children celebrating Guy Fawkes Night or Bonfire Night on November 5. Catherine was the patron saint of unmarried girls and philosophers and is fondly remembered in Canada because of Marguerite Bourgeoys, who founded the Congregation of Notre Dame and opened the first Canadian school in 1658.

Marguerite encouraged her students to pull taffy on this day in Catherine's honour. In the boarding schools of the sisters of the Congregation of Notre Dame, the pupils still carry out the tradition and share with the sisters a delicious molasses candy, which in French is called *la tire* and is pronounced *lah teer*. The custom spread to all of French Canada, and spinsters over twenty-five years of age implored good St. Catherine's aid as they made this traditional candy.[1]

Legend tells us that Marguerite made the taffy from molasses and any other ingredients she could find to lure her students to school. From *Traditional Quebec Cooking*, we have a recipe for this very special treat:

TIRE STE-CATHERINE

1 cup sugar
1 cup brown sugar
½ cup dark corn syrup
1 tablespoon vinegar

La Tire Ste-Catherine

1 cup molasses
1 teaspoon butter
1 teaspoon baking soda

Place all ingredients except the soda in a medium saucepan. Cook and stir on medium heat until boiling. Cook on medium heat without stirring until temperature reaches 264 degrees Fahrenheit on a candy thermometer. Remove from heat, add sifted baking soda and mix well. Pour into 3 or 4 greased pie plates and cool until lukewarm. To pull taffy, generously butter hands and pull until it is two feet long, fold in two and pull again until it becomes a beige colour. Stretch in a long rope one inch thick and cut in one inch lengths. Wrap each candy in wax paper.[2]

St. Catherine's Day was also designated as the feast day to honour women over the age of twenty-five who were still unmarried. They were often considered too old to wed as they were "old maids" or "unclaimed treasures." The tradition developed of wearing a green dress (the colour of hope) and an elaborately decorated hat and walking out in search of a husband. In some communities matchmaking balls were held during the evening of November 25 for all the single women who wanted to marry. The oldest woman at the ball had the honour of putting a crown on St. Catherine's statue.

Traditions, customs, and superstitions that relate to love and marriage were a part of everyday life in all the countries and societies around the world. Some of these customs took root here in Canada as young people focused on the vital question: "Who will I marry?" Even little girls used daisies to learn whether "He loves me" or "He loves me not." Apples were believed to have the power to foretell the future. You placed apple seeds on your knuckles or a cheek and named each one after a boy. The seed that stayed on the longest was destined to be your future husband! Young girls also slept with pieces of wedding cake under their pillows in the hope of dreaming of their future husbands.

The bees that were so common in Canada in the early years were actually a perfect reason for courting couples to get together without a chaperone. At apple-paring bees a girl attempted to cut the peel off the fruit in one long piece and then toss it over her shoulder. The letter that it formed when it fell on the floor was the first letter of the girl's future husband's name.

Corn-husking bees gave young men the opportunity to kiss their partners every time a red ear of corn appeared. Box socials and pie socials, popular in many communities across Canada, were organized as fundraisers, but also provided an opportunity for courting couples to meet. Women baked the pies or decorated a box filled with lunch for two people and smuggled it into the hall, church, school, or wherever the event was to take place. Then the pies or boxes were auctioned to the men. Fierce competition ensued as the young men each bid to eat supper with the girl he cared about and walk her home after the event.

Finally, the young man would ask the girl's father or guardian for permission to marry her, and if an affirmative answer was received, the date could be set. This was often a problem, for in the early days of settlement there were few clergymen, so a military officer or a justice of the peace might be pressed into service. Weddings close to Christmas Day were popular since they were usually held at home and family members had often travelled long distances to share the food and fellowship of the day. The traditional meal or tea following the ceremony could range from elaborate to the simple, hearty fare prepared by the family. Frances Stewart of Douro Township in Peterborough County describes the simple reception following her daughter's wedding in May 1848 in a letter to her sister, Catherine, in Ireland:

> The ceremony was performed about six o'clock in the evening, as we thought having tea soon after would give us some occupation.... Anna and Ellen presided at the tea table at one end of the room, and poured out tea and coffee which the boys handed

about, as the party sat in groups in different parts of the room. In the middle was a table with bread and butter, buttered buns, plum cake, little shrewsbury cakes and some other kind....

The bride's cake was cut up. It too was home made and ornamented with coloured comfits [sweetmeats] and just as good and rich looking as any store bought plum cake.

All this kept us busy until candle light, and at 9 o'clock we had some nice singing and playing ... we had a little supper: cold fowl, and some lamb, and some ham, and salad, and some tarts — and raisins almonds — and apples — and etc., and etc., and etc.

The bride and bridegroom's healths were drunk, the gentlemen having glasses of punch, the ladies wine.

After more merriment and well wishing by friends and family the groom changed into a warmer and commoner suit and got his wagon ready for the journey to their new home. With help from the other women, the bride packed up her trunks and parcels, climbed aboard the wagon and by one o'clock in the morning they were off.

Within a day or two the young couple could expect to be awakened from sleep as the men of their community assembled old pots and kettles for a charivari. Also known as a shivaree, it was a common practice across Canada in rural areas and only ended when the young couple invited the noisemakers into their home for refreshments, or the groom gave them money for a treat at the local inn or tavern where they could drink a toast to the happy couple. This custom of serenading newly married couples may have come from Europe in the Middle Ages, but many historians believe it originated in Lower Canada, since it appears to have been first mentioned in the *Quebec Gazette* on January 12, 1786.[3]

30

St. Andrew:
The Man and the Society

We look to Scotland for all our ideas of civilization.

— Voltaire

November 30 is remembered as the Day of St. Andrew, the patron saint of Scotland, Russia, and fishermen. Andrew, himself a fisherman in the village of Bethsaida in Galilee, is believed to be the first disciple called by Jesus Christ. Along with his brother, Simon Peter, he was always eager to bring new followers to his master. It was St. Andrew who pointed out the young boy with the five loaves and two fishes with which Jesus fed the crowd of five thousand who had gathered to listen to his preaching on that fateful day.

Andrew travelled extensively to preach the Christian gospel until November 30, 60 A.D., when he was arrested for his Christian beliefs and tried by a Roman governor. He was crucified on a diagonal cross, and a white diagonal cross on a blue field became the flag of St. Andrew. The same emblem forms a part of the Union Jack. It is believed his body was buried on the coast of Fife, where the city of St. Andrew grew and the cathedral of St. Andrew was later built.

How did Andrew become a saint? There is a Scottish legend that in 832 A.D. Scotland was conceived and Andrew became its patron saint as the result of a battle fought and won in the Vale of Piffer in present-day East Lothian. King Angus of Albannach and King Eochaidh the Poisonous of the Dalriadan Scots joined forces against the Saxons, who attacked them and at first appeared to be winning. Suddenly, Angus saw a white cloud formation in the shape of a saltire (a St. Andrew's cross), and both kings pledged to make Andrew their patron saint if he gave them the victory. From that victory, eventually a nation was born and a saint was confirmed.

St. Andrew became the last harvest saint of the liturgical year, and in ancient times each animal had its slaughtering days in November as families prepared for the long, dark, cold winter ahead. Sheep were assigned to St. Andrew, which would have been an honour since they were esteemed for their unique fivefold value: fleece, milk, meat, manure, and skin (whose special character made it a writing material of incomparable durability). In addition, Singed Sheep's Head became a national Scottish dish in St. Andrew's honour, while Haggis became a mandatory item at any meal recognizing the saint whenever and wherever Scots travelled around the world.

The Cook and Housewife's Manual: A Practical System of Modern Domestic Cookery and Family Management by Mistress Margaret Dods, published in Edinburgh in 1829, provides a suggested menu for just such a meal:

BILL OF FARE FOR ST. ANDREW'S DAY, BURN'S CLUBS OR OTHER SCOTTISH NATIONAL DINNERS

FIRST COURSE
Friar's Chicken or Scotch Brown Soup
(*Remove* Braised Turkey)

Brown Fricassee or Duck   Potted Game   Minced Collops
Salt Cod with Egg Sauce   Haggis   Crimped Skate
Remove Chicken Pie

Smoked Tongue   Tripe in White Fricassee

Salt Caithness Goose, or Solan Goose
Sheep's-Head Broth
(*Remove* Two Tups' Head and Trotters)
(*Remove* Haunch of Venison or Mutton
with Wine Sauce and Currant Jelly)

St. Andrew

SECOND COURSE
Roast Fowls, with *Drappit* Egg,
or Lamb's Head Dressed

Buttered Partans   Small Pastry   Stewed Onions

Calf's Feet Jelly   Rich Eating Posset   Blancmange

in a China Punch Bowl

Apple-Puddings in Skins   Small Pastry   Plum-Damas Pie

A Black Cock, or Three Ptarmigan.[1]

The St. Andrew's Society of Montreal, formed in 1835, celebrated with an Anniversary Ball and Dinner at the Windsor Hotel on November 30, 1887. The Bill of Fare included Oysters, Canadian Soup, Fillet of Beef Garnished, Roast Chicken in Moulds, Game Pie with Truffles, Goose Liver Pie Strasburg Style, Pyramids of Jellied Turkey, Lobster with Herbs, Haggis, Roasted Turkey, Chicken, Beef, Partridge, Prairie Hen, Black Duck, and Quail. There were Lobster, Chicken, and Vegetable Salads, and to conclude the dinner there was a choice of Macaroon, Nougat or Fruit Pyramids, Swiss Cake, Frozen Meringues, Confectionery, Neapolitan Ice Cream, Fruit, and Coffee. Truly an anniversary dinner to remember![2]

The St. Andrew's Society of Toronto was established in 1836 and incorporated on October 30, 1886, under the Benevolent and Provident Societies Act with the following purposes:

> The purposes of the Society are to render assistance and grant relief to natives of Scotland, resident in Canada, their spouses, widows, widowers and their descendants who may be in want or distress, and in other deserving cases recommended by the Chaplains of the Society or the Managers; and to preserve and foster the Scottish heritage and an understanding of contemporary life in Scotland.

Membership wasn't limited to those of Scottish ancestry but was, and is, inclusive: "Scots, descendants of Scots and those who support the objectives of the Society are eligible for membership in the Society." The Constitution reminds the members that: "The Society shall hold an Anniversary Assembly on St. Andrew's Day, or on such other day as may be determined by the Executive Council."

The societies, created to assist newly arrived Scots, were surprised to find they were involved in a maelstrom of political activity in the late 1840s after the arrival of James Bruce, Earl of Elgin and Kincardine, and newly appointed governor general. Soon after his arrival, the Toronto society elected him an honorary patron and member in August 1847. When, in April 1849, he signed the Rebellion Losses Bill to compensate those who had suffered property damage in Lower Canada during the 1837–38 Rebellions, he was pelted with stones and refuse as he returned from the Legislature. A few days later he was assaulted again, and the patriotic societies in Montreal revoked his memberships. The St. Andrew's Society in Montreal "resolved to return His Excellency's subscription of £10 with interest from the day of payment."

The St. Andrew's Society of Toronto responded to this outrage with an address of loyalty and praise presented to His Excellency on October 9, when one hundred and eighty strong and led by three pipers, they marched to Mrs. Ellah's Hotel at 72 King Street West for the ceremony. Lord Elgin concluded his remarks by requesting "that he have the pleasure of shaking hands with every member of the Society, which was done."

In 1857 the Toronto society received "a Ram's Head Snuff-Mull, most magnificently mounted," a gift from John Ewart, the president. Despite the superb gift, a reminder of the very origins of the celebration, this was a year of severe depression in British North America. Trade was so depressed and money was so scarce that the society was overwhelmed with requests for assistance. Each member was asked to "subscribe ten shillings or such other funds as he may find convenient," and by February the following year £90 had been collected.

The society also supported and contributed to the soup kitchen operated by the House of Industry. Due to the economy, it was decided that the ball and dinner wouldn't be held in 1858. That was the year William Lyon Mackenzie, the first mayor of Toronto and the leader of the 1837 Rebellion, was elected a member, to be followed by a number of other well-known political figures — Sir John A. Macdonald, George Brown, and Sir Oliver Mowat, who was a member from 1842 to his death in 1903.

Sir Oliver may have been in attendance in 1896 when indeed the society and its members were again ready to celebrate as described in "The Nicht 1896":

> On November 30, 1896, the St. Andrew's Society of Toronto held its St. Andrew's Ball to celebrate the Society's sixtieth anniversary. The next day, Tuesday, December 1, the Toronto newspapers gave extensive coverage of the ball. The headline on the front page of the *Globe* read, "Opening Event of the Social Season: a Grand Success." In its article the *Mail* declared, "in point of excellence of arrangements, numbers in attendance, and beauty of decoration (the Ball) may be fairly said to have eclipsed anything of the kind ever before attempted by the Society.... It is of notable character of the St. Andrew's Society that whatever it does it does well ... whether in arrangement ... of such a social event ... or in the work of extending of

helping hand to the struggling and bearing comfort to destitute homes."

Over seven hundred guests were in attendance, including the Guests of Honour, the Governor General and Lady Aberdeen. Other honoured guests included Lieutenant Governor Kirkpatrick, Mayor Fleming, the Honourable Chief Justice Hagarty, the Presidents of the St. Andrew's Society in Montreal, Winnipeg, Illinois, and San Francisco, as well as the Toronto Presidents of the Caledonian Society, the Sons of Scotland, the Gaelic Society and the St. George's Society.

The Old Pavilion, the site of the ball, had been transformed, in the words of the *Mail* "a veritable bower of beauty." From the lengthy descriptions in the newspapers we learn that a huge St. Andrew's Cross covered the ceiling. From its edges alternate streamers of red and white curved to the upper windows "forming a rich and striking canopy over the whole room." The railing of the top gallery was draped with blue and white, two flags hung from each pillar, and from the gasaliers on each pillar were long folds of red, white and blue bunting. In the middle of the west side, the Royal Arms of Scotland were surrounded with the Royal Stuart Tartan and above them the Imperial Arms of Great Britain were draped in red, white and blue. The walls of the first gallery were decorated in red and the coat of arms of the provinces. On the main floor the pillars were covered in tartan of crossed claymores.

A stage with settees, palms, and chrysanthemums was arranged for those who wish to sit. The *Mail's* observation that "on either side of the stage the four banners of the society were displayed, gold on a black silk ground, and on a table stood one of the most prized treasures of the society, the great snuff mull ..." [This, of course, was the "Rams Head Snuff Mull, most magnificently mounted," the gift of John Ewart in 1857.]

The Dancing commenced at 9:00 p.m. with the Opening March led by the Pipers. The programme card, "a Scottish thistle design with a heavy gilt border and a representation of St. Andrew," indicated that there were twenty-seven dances — Vales, Two Steps, Lancers, Reel o'Tulloch, Scotch Reels, a Highland Scottisch, and a Polka. A bugler sounded a call before each dance and the music was provided by the "the excellent band of the 48th Highlanders." At midnight a meal was served after which the dancing was resumed. The only information we have about the meal was that it was catered by a firm called Webb and the wines were supplied by Michie and Company.

All in all, the evening must have been a huge success. The *Globe*'s correspondent was impressed with the attention to detail, commented admiringly on "the spirit of good fellowship which is characteristic of Scottish celebrations," and was most decidedly of the opinion that the Society "may fairly claim that the St. Andrew's Ball is the social function, par excellence, of the season."[3]

Feast of Dedication:
Hanukkah or Chanukah

*May the lights of Hanukkah usher in a
better world for all humankind.*

The celebration of Hanukkah, the Festival of Lights, is one of the happiest of Jewish holidays. It usually falls in the period from late November to early January and lasts eight days. Hanukkah is a commemoration of a miracle that happened in Palestine more than two thousand years ago. At that time the Syrian Greeks were rulers of the land and had outlawed the Jewish faith. They took over the Jewish Temple in Jerusalem, erected altars and the idols they worshipped, and renamed the Temple after their god Zeus.

Feast of Dedication

After years of bitter fighting, the Jews won a number of victories over the armies of the Syrian king and were able to recapture the Temple. They were determined to cleanse it and dedicate it once again to the One God. When the cleansing was completed and it was time to kindle the eternal light in the Temple lamp, they could only find a small jar of sanctified oil. This was just enough to keep the eternal light before the Holy Ark burning for one day.

They needed enough for eight days, since it took that long to make more oil. What to do? They poured a few drops of oil from the one precious container into one of the eight cups of the Temple lamp, called the Menorah, and lit it. Miraculously, when they returned the next day, the wick was still burning brightly. Each day they added a few drops more until the eight cups of the Menorah were alight. There was much to celebrate — victory over their enemies, the temple cleansed, and the miracle of the oil!

Again for new arrivals in Canada of Jewish ancestry and faith, this miracle would be one of their most precious memories. To honour this memory, families would use a special candle holder, or *channukkiyah*, that holds eight candles, plus one more, the *shammash* (a "worker" or "servant" candle). On the first night the *shammash* is lit and used to light the first candle, which is usually in the middle. On the second night the *shammash* is lit and then used to light two candles, and so on, for eight days of celebration.

This is a time of good food and fellowship. Potato latkes cooked in oil are a favourite, since they are symbols of the miracle of the oil. In Canada they are often served with apple-sauce and sour cream. Doughnuts and chocolate (wrapped in gold foil) called *gelt* are treats enjoyed by children.

LATKES
(POTATO PANCAKES)

4–5 large grated raw potatoes
1 medium onion
2 eggs
½ teaspoon baking powder
1½ teaspoons salt
dash pepper
¼ cup flour or matzo meal

Combine all ingredients. If a food processor is used, a grater is unnecessary. Drop by tablespoonful into hot vegetable oil which is almost deep enough to cover pancakes. Fry over moderate heat until brown on one side. Turn and brown other side. Drain on paper towel. Serves 4–6.[1]

Latkes may be served with a number of toppings, including applesauce. Here is a variation that is delicious:

APPLE PEAR SAUCE

6 apples, peeled, chopped (Royal Gala, Golden Delicious, or Empire)
6 ripe pears, peeled, chopped (Bartlett or Bosc)
½ cup brown sugar
1 tablespoon lemon juice
1 teaspoon cinnamon
pinch each of nutmeg, allspice, ginger
½ cup apple juice

Combine apples, pears, brown sugar, lemon juice, and spices in a Dutch oven. Bring to a boil, cover and simmer gently for about 45 minutes. Uncover and cook, stirring often, until sauce is as thick as you like. Apples and pears will be quite soft, but if you want a very smooth sauce purée it. Makes about 3 to 4 cups.[2]

The children are given small square spinning tops to play a game called *dreydel* that have on their sides the Hebrew letters NGHS. These letters stand for the words: *Nes Godol Hoyoh Shom*, meaning "a great miracle happened here."

Christ's Mass

Christmas gift suggestions:
To your enemy, forgiveness.
To an opponent, tolerance.
To a friend, your heart.
To a customer, service.
To all, charity.
To every child, a good example.
To yourself, respect.

— Oren Arnold

For centuries many Christians around the world have celebrated the birth of Christ in December or early January. There is no historical record of the actual date of this event that occurred more than two thousand years ago, but in 336 A.D. the Christian Church decreed that Christ's Mass, or Christmas, would be celebrated on December 25.

At that time in history it was thought that December 25 was the shortest day of the year, and over the centuries many beliefs, traditions, and customs of the ancient winter solstice festival became part of the celebration. People believed that the winter solstice was the beginning of the sun's return journey. They welcomed the occasion with the exchange of gifts, the playing of music, singing, and the gathering of families to enjoy rich food. As with many other celebrations, these activities were incorporated into the new Christian festival.

Newcomers from around the world arrived in colonial Canada with a multitude of beliefs, superstitions, traditions, and observances. These customs didn't all focus on one date, but the celebration has evolved into a blending of the rituals of many people and many lands. Sometimes newcomers have been influenced by their new neighbours and friends and have integrated new customs into their own depending on the community where they settled.

Advent is a time of preparation for the observance of the Nativity or Christmas. It begins on the Sunday nearest November 30 and includes the four Sundays leading to Christmas Day. The first Sunday in Advent is known as "Stir-up Sunday" guided by a Bible reading in the old Anglican prayer book that begins "Stir-up, we beseech thee O Lord, the hearts of thy faithful people." This is the traditional day to make plum or carrot puddings, fruit cakes, and minced meat for Christmas feasts and for the long winter ahead. Tokens were added to the puddings to predict the fortunes of the family members such as coins, rings, thimbles, and buttons. Legend and folklore tells us that everyone in the family took a turn at stirring from eldest to youngest, and always stirring from left to right in honour of the Three Wise Men arriving from east to west.

In Acadia it is believed that cold weather for Advent indicates a mild winter, while a mild Advent will bring a long, cold, hard winter.[1] In some homes, churches, and communities, candles are lit, processions held, and special treats prepared and enjoyed. Among the treats were small cakes and cookies often cut or moulded and baked in the shape of animals that shared their stable with the baby Jesus. Gingerbread wafers or cookies might be made to decorate the family tree, just as Queen Victoria did, for her subjects knew "she loved her candlelit Christmas tree with the gingerbread decorations."[2]

The tradition of cutting and bringing a live tree indoors is attributed to Martin Luther, and Queen Victoria's tree was introduced to her and the children by her German-born husband, Albert. Long before her birth, however, the tradition of a decorated indoor tree had reached the shores of British North America, for we learn that:

The first decorated Christmas tree in Canada was erected in Sorel, Quebec, in 1781, by Major-General Friedrich-Adolphus von Riedesel. Riedesel was commander of the "Hessian troops" fighting the American Revolution and he had come to Canada with his wife and family (one of his daughters was christened "Canada"). Amongst others, those present at the illumination of the first Christmas tree were: Prince Edward, the Duke of Richmond; Captain Charles Peel, the Count and the Countess of Dalhousie. The house still exists and in 1966, the German-Canadian Alliance unveiled a bronze plaque on which is engraved:

In this house, a Christmas tree was lit by General von Riedesel on the 25th December 1781 in German tradition, which is recorded as the first Christmas tree in Canada.[3]

Many cultural groups, including Dutch, German, Belgian, Serbian, and Russian, celebrate St. Nicholas Day or Sinterklaas Day in early December. It is believed that St. Nicholas was born in the province of Lycia in Asia Minor in the third century. The son of very rich parents, he gave his inheritance to the poor and became known for his good works, kindness, and concern for orphaned children, and also for the miracles he performed. He was chosen bishop of Myra and became the patron saint of children, sailors in distress, and marriageable maidens.[4]

St. Nicholas Day, December 6, is one of the most popular celebrations for Canadians of Dutch ancestry, for their legends have the saint arriving on a horse with a Moorish boy, Black Peter, walking beside him and carrying a bag of toys for good children and switches for naughty ones. The children leave their shoes on the doorstep with treats for the horse such as hay and carrots. Their gifts may appear in their shoes or in unusual containers such as hollowed-out cabbages. Some Dutch families went to great lengths to disguise the gifts. They would wrap them, coat them with dough, and then bake them in the oven to make them look like loaves of bread![5]

Newcomers from Holland, Germany, Russia, Serbia, and Belgium likely brought St. Nicholas traditions with them when they arrived in Canada. In the late nineteenth and early twentieth centuries, Belgian settlers in Manitoba not only had memories of St. Nicholas but knew recipes for age-old treats such as Speculaas, which were served on his day. These are the national cookies of Flanders and are an important addition to this feast day. Ingredients include butter, dark brown sugar, egg, cinnamon, flour, and baking powder and are very similar to the *spekulatius* of the Netherlands and northern Germany.[6]

Meanwhile in British Columbia we learn that by the late 1870s there were four hundred Chinese cooks and servants in Victoria providing the only domestic services available to the well-to-do. At Christmas time a group of these cooks who knew each other well would congregate during evenings at one employer's house after another and have co-operative Christmas cake decorating bees. The results were fantastic, with stiff white sugar pagodas, et cetera ... on the tops of the cakes.[7]

December for most of our ancestors living in Canada would have been a time not only of preparations but of anticipation. The gathering of family members and the fellowship and sharing of favourite foods held great religious significance for many families. This was also a preferred time for weddings, as family members travelling by horse and sleigh, or in the early twentieth century by newfangled cars, were already assembled and conveniently on hand.

Many Christians went to Confession on Christmas Eve and attended Midnight Mass. This was a fast day for them, and meals were made from fish and vegetables. The fast before the feast whetted the appetite so that Christmas Day dinner was appreciated all the more.

The traditions of Acadians living in Prince Edward Island have survived for decades:

> Midnight Mass drew everyone to church;
> those who lived nearby walked and those from
> further away travelled by sleigh. If the night
> was dark each sleigh would have a lantern to

light the way. Afterwards the congregation was soon homeward bound for the *réveillon*. Everyone looked forward to this traditional meal, especially since for many it marked the end of four weeks of penance when fast and abstinence were the order of the day. *Pâté* (meat pie) was always greatly appreciated, and especially rabbit pie. Often the *réveillon* was the first chance people had to taste the delicious blood pudding prepared during Advent when the pigs were slaughtered.

The *réveillon* was for the most part a family celebration but sometimes neighbours, relatives and friends would gather together. If there were musicians in a crowd, music and song added to the fun.

Christmas in those days was centered more on the children, and they were the only ones who received gifts. On Christmas Eve the children hung their stockings near the chimney where St. Nicholas would find them and fill them with goodies. They would find them filled with treats — an apple, or sometimes only half an apple, a hard-boiled egg, a few hard candies, and an orange for the more fortunate children. Later the children would visit their godparents who always had a special Christmas present for them — usually a gingerbread man.

The main dish for Christmas dinner was always some type of stuffed fowl — very often goose. The dessert could vary, but steamed pudding was always popular. As for sweets, they were not as abundant then as they are today. However, *croiquignoles*, a kind of deep-fried bread, pork tarts and several kinds of cookies were served. *Pâté* was always a popular festival dish. People enjoyed it at the *réveillon*, and it was served for breakfast and for supper on Christmas day. Christmas afternoon, the families used to take the children to the church to visit the Christ child's crib.

All in all, Acadian Christmas celebrations were a family affair with celebrations of simple yet religious nature, much as the Christmas of all Islanders, taking its beauty from great simplicity and appreciation for family and friends.[8]

For French Canadians in Quebec their feast also began as soon as they returned from Midnight Mass. This *réveillon* brings family and friends to a groaning table with *tourtière* the centrepiece of the meal. This meat pie with potatoes, onions, and seasonings is named for the dish in which it is baked — the *tourte*.

We learn that in Newfoundland "the old custom is that Christmas Celebrations begin on Christmas Eve, with a Thanksgiving meal of salt fish followed by sweet raisin bread called 'Christmas Fruit Loaf.' Fishing was the means of livelihood and so fish had its place in thanksgiving before the day of the feasting."[9]

Christmas dinner in Newfoundland was a special family get-together. The best of the garden produce was kept in the root cellar for this occasion. The meal consisted of roast beef, rabbit or seabirds, served with salt beef, cabbage, turnips, carrots, parsnips, potatoes, Figgy Duff, and Pease Pudding. Steamed Suet Pudding was served with rum sauce as dessert. Since this was the only time during the year that fishermen could relax, they began preparations in the fall, bartering for coarse salt and enough contraband rum to celebrate the twelve days of Christmas.[10]

For many families the Christmas feast was held at midday, and though we may have visions of that elegant meal, the reality might have been quite different depending on where a family lived. Florence Howey was the new bride of Dr. William Howey when he was hired by the Canadian Pacific Railway in 1882 to look after the working gangs, construction crews, and staff at headquarters camps along the route under construction. They were stationed at present-day Sudbury in remote

Northern Ontario. The year was 1883, and the railway (the only access by land to the rest of the province and the world) had just reached their log house, provided by the CPR:

> December now, and Christmas is in the offing. The track has reached here in November and more luxuries were available, at least what seemed luxuries after our long subsistence on absolute necessities, therefore we decided to give a party. To our delight Dr. Girdwood had sent up some turkeys for us and the patients in the hospital. Then the question arose, whom shall we invite. The engineers whose homes were in Canada had gone to spend Christmas with their families. Mr. Wiley (of the cold baths) and Mr. Shaw the big Scotsman, whose homes were across the sea had left, but there were several nice fellows who could not leave and were looking kind of homesick, so our list was made up, Gough and Harry Fairman, bookkeeper and clerk in the Company's store, Francis Fulford, Draftsman Pierre, Mueler, Commissariat for the boarding cars, and Mr. Thompson who was in charge of the supply store, his little boy was with him. They had expected to go home but were unable to do

so. We must ask Miss Horrigan, the only girl available. These and ourselves counted up made eleven, our table accompanied eight comfortably; but we thought that by distributing the fat and lean guests judiciously, and by sitting very close together on the benches we might manage four on each side, I would have one windsor chair at the head of the table, and with doctor on a box at the foot, and little Billy Thompson on a box at the corner, by his father, we might manage. So they were all invited and all came. Miss Horrigan came the previous day and she and Pierre undertook the decorations, and made a woodland bower of our little room, with cedar and balsam boughs. They prided themselves on a "Merry Christmas" done with cedar which extended nearly the length of one log on one side of the room. It was very much admired, until little Billy, in a rather loud whisper said to his father, "Pa see that S." We all looked at that "S" and discovered for the first time that it was hind side before. Then as usual, pride had a fall. When dinner was ready there was a discussion as to who should sit where. Someone suggested measuring each guest to determine the amount of bench space they would require, and then space off the benches accordingly. However, that idea was not carried out. Imagine us then, I in our one chair at the head, doctor on a box at the foot and our guests rubbing elbows at each side. There was no room on the table for the turkey, so Pierre volunteered to carve it in the kitchen, but after we were seated he brought it in carrying the platter high and marched solemnly around the table, proclaiming about St. Nicholas and a turkey, until the company protested that they would rather eat it than hear about it. Despite the many makeshifts, which we did not mind at all, it was a real Christmas dinner with most of the eatments and drinkments which custom and tradition have made almost necessities. All were in good spirits although we were a little bunch of strangers gathered from every direction, away back in the wilderness, hundreds of miles from any of our kin and friends. One would not feel so isolated now where the distance in annihilated by planes and fast trains. If any one had spoken of travelling by air it would have been a joke too silly to laugh at. Before our guests departed we sang Auld Lang Syne, I think everyone, as we sang, visioned a different group of old acquaintances, and it seemed to cast just a little shade of sadness, which soon passed and as they said "good night" everyone agreed that we'd had a very Merry Christmas.[11]

33

Season of Celebrations

Now, now the mirth comes
With the cake full of plums,
Where Beane's the King of the sport here;
Beside we must know,
The Pea also
Must revell, as Queene, in the Court here.

— Robert Herrick, "Twelfth Night, or King and Queen"

Beginning on Christmas Day and ending on Epiphany, Canadians could be involved in a series of celebrations, depending on country of origin, religious beliefs, their community, or their calendar. As December 25 approached, homes and places of worship were decorated, special foods were prepared, and gifts were made by hand and tucked away in secret places. For many families this was the start of a round of social events marking the Twelve Days of Christmas and culminating on Epiphany on January 6.

In the meantime, however, the Festival of St. John the Evangelist on December 27 wasn't forgotten, as we learn that

> the two lodges of masons in Newark, although their regular meetings were held in the Freemasons' Hall occasionally marched in procession, often accompanied by a band, to one of the taverns for dinner to celebrate such special occasions as the Festival of St. John the Evangelist on 27 December. The account book of York's earliest innkeeper, Abner Miles, records charging each guest at a St. John's dinner in his inn, 16 shillings per person in 1795.[1]

On Boxing Day the custom of "mummering" was practised in many communities in Newfoundland and Labrador. Young people dressed in weird costumes were called mummers in Newfoundland and jannies in Labrador. They went from house to house, often walking in without knocking, and looking for treats. The youths could be served homemade cookies such as jam jams, molasses or coconut, molasses candy, sweet bread, or Christmas cake, and Purity sweet syrup or home-brew if they were adults.[2] They might sing or dance or play musical instruments such as fiddles or accordions. Some older groups staged short plays, and in this way kept alive a historic English folk tradition. Many people believe there is a strong link between mummers and jannies and the Hogmanay visits of children in Scottish communities.

January 5 has been known as Twelfth Night, the Eve of Epiphany, the Day of the Three Kings, Little Christmas, and Old Christmas. Old Christmas is perhaps the most accurate for, by the Julian or Old Style Calendar that some churches still follow for their feast days, Christmas comes on this day and Epiphany falls on January 19.

Epiphany is described as "the occasion on which Jesus appeared to the Magi" in the Book of Matthew in the Bible, or "a moment of sudden and great revelation or understanding." The Magi, or Three Wise Men from the East, brought gifts of gold, frankincense, and myrrh to the infant. The gifts of frank-incense and myrrh were as precious as gold in biblical times. Frankincense is a resin with a strong scent of balsam that was used by the ancients for embalming. Myrrh is also an aromatic resin prized as a perfume, a spice, and a medicine. It was once worn on the crowns of Persian kings to symbolize their wealth.[3]

Epiphany, celebrated on January 6, really honours three very special events: the adoration of the Magi, Christ's baptism in the Jordan River by John the Baptist, and the Miracle of Cana when Jesus turned six pots of water into wine to serve the guests at a wedding feast. That was the first miracle performed by Jesus and was done at the request of Mary, his mother.

In preparation for this celebration, many special foods were prepared. French housewives baked Twelfth Night Cake containing a pea and a bean and whoever found them was assured of good fortune in the coming year and were declared the King of the Bean and Queen of the Pea and presided over the festivities.

TWELFTH NIGHT CAKE

1 cup butter at room temperature
1 cup granulated sugar
2 eggs
1 tablespoon orange peel
1 tablespoon lemon peel
2½ cups all purpose flour
2 teaspoons baking powder
1 teaspoon baking soda
½ teaspoon salt
1 cup buttermilk
½ cup chopped walnuts or pecans
1 dried pea and 1 dried bean

Glaze

⅓ cup granulated sugar
¼ cup orange juice
1 teaspoon rum
1 teaspoon lemon juice

In a large bowl, cream powder and sugar. Add eggs, orange and lemon peel; beat well. In a separate bowl, combine flour, baking powder, soda, and salt. Add dry ingredients to creamed mixture alternately with buttermilk, beating until smooth. Stir in glace fruit, nuts, and pea and bean. Spoon into well-greased 10-inch cube angel food cake pan. Bake in preheated 350-degree oven 55 to 60 minutes or until cake tester inserted in centre comes out clean.

Meanwhile, in small saucepan, combine glaze ingredients and bring to boil. Remove from heat; slowly pour over cake in pan. Let cake stand 24 hours before removing and serving.

Makes 12 to 16 servings.[4]

Traditionally, the favourite beverage for the celebration was Lamb's Wool. This was a hot, alcoholic drink that Samuel Pepys and many of his contemporaries favoured. It was made of hot ale, sweetened with sugar, thickened with crushed, roasted apples, and flavoured with nutmeg or ground ginger.[5]

For Canadians of Ukrainian or Eastern Orthodox ancestry, Christmas was celebrated on January 7, as their churches follow the Julian calendar. The evening before, January 6, families celebrate with a Holy Supper of twelve meatless dishes in honour of the twelve apostles. This was often the culmination of forty days of fasting when meat and dairy products were banned. The meal begins when the children in the family see the first star. The father, or head of the family, then places a sheaf of wheat in the room where they will feast to symbolize the gathering of the family. The head of the family then tastes the Kutia, made from boiled wheat, poppy seeds, honey, and nuts. This first meatless dish must then be tasted by everyone because it symbolizes family unity and prosperity. After Midnight Mass, the fast is over and the feast begins!

34

New Year's Eve and Hogmanay

Ring out the old, ring in the new,
Ring, happy bells, across the snow:
The year is going, let him go;

Ring out the false, ring in the true.

— Alfred Tennyson, "Ring Out, Wild Bells"

A s the old year draws to a close, it is a time of celebration in most of the homes and communities in Canada. Many traditions, beliefs, and superstitions surround the last day of the old year and the arrival of the New Year as the clock strikes midnight.

For French Canadians it is an evening of visiting and socializing. "La Giugnolée," an old French song, is often sung about the fellowship and the visits and gifts of mistletoe, *qui*, in French. Often the visitors collect gifts of money, food, and clothing for poor families.

In many homes it is a time to foretell the future by using the Bible. With eyes closed, the Bible is opened and the right forefinger is placed at random on the page. The words will tell whether it will be a happy year or one of hardship.

For Scottish Canadians the celebration of New Year's Eve or Hogmanay is the highlight of their year. Often called Cake Day in Scotland, it is a day that demands much advance preparation by the cooks, chefs, bakers, and housewives who plan to entertain. Weeks in advance traditional dishes such as Black Bun (also known as Scotch Currant Plum Cake) are prepared. This is always a surprise for anyone tasting it for the first time, since it actually looks like a pie. It is believed to have originated in Scottish bakeries when they were only allowed to make cakes for special holidays, so they would set aside a lump of bread dough to which dried fruit and spices were added. Because this rich mixture wouldn't stay together, it was enclosed in a very thin casing of bread dough and baked. Through the years this has become a casing of rich, short pastry.

The Hogmanay table always includes shortbread, which is often shaped in a large circle, with the edges notched with thumb and forefinger to symbolize the sun's rays, a custom that has survived for centuries. Loaves of oaten bread and oatcakes with soft cheese are also prepared in advance for the children going door to door looking for treats on the last day of the old year. They wrap themselves in sheets, double them up in front to form pockets, and then start chanting:

> Hogmanay,
> Trolloday!
> Get up good housewives and shake
> Your feathers,
> And dinna think that we are
> Beggars;
> For we are bairns come out to play,
> Get up and gie's our Hogmanay.
> My feet's cauld, my shoon's thin;
> Gie's my cake, and let me rin.

Other treats prepared for this night are Scots Eggs or Scotch Eggs, and of course Haggis.

In Cape Breton cookies called Hogmanay Rich Biscuits are made for special occasions throughout the year, but are a "must" for this night. When they are cool, they are spread with strawberry jam or lemon cheese. On New Year's Eve they are arranged on a silver cake plate and served with ginger wine.

HOGMANAY RICH BISCUITS

2 eggs, separated
½ cup sugar
1 teaspoon lemon flavouring
½ cup flour
¼ teaspoon salt

Beat the egg whites until stiff. Add the sugar
and the flavouring. Beat the egg yolks well
and add to the egg white mixture. Add flour
and salt last. Drop on a buttered cookie sheet
by tablespoonfuls. Leave room for the cookies to rise and expand. Bake for 15 minutes at
425 degrees. Yield about 24 cookies.[1]

Ginger wine is only one of the many spirits served to
guests on this night in Scottish homes. Others great favourites
include: Atholl Brose, a mixture of whisky, honey, oatmeal,
and cream; Auld Man's Milk, a combination of eggs, sugar,
cream, and whisky; and Het Pint, a blend of ale, whisky, sugar,
eggs, and nutmeg, slowly warmed, constantly stirred, and
poured between pan and mug until it froths.

As well as the advance preparations for food and beverages,
Scottish Canadians brought with them the belief that before
the old year ended they must pay all their bills, make peace

with their enemies, clean the house, barns, and outbuildings, mend their clothes, and return any tools or equipment borrowed from their friends and neighbours.

With the clock ticking toward midnight, anticipation mounts about who will be the "first foot" to cross the threshold. It was, and still is, believed that this person determines the fortune of the family for the coming year. The hope is that it will be a man, tall with dark hair, and that he will be carrying gifts, including whisky, tea, coal, or salt, symbols of good health, good fortune, good luck, a warm home, and a full larder.

This is another occasion when, in the wee small hours of the morning, before the guests leave, the tradition of joining hands and singing "Auld Lang Syne" must not be forgotten.

Notes

Preface

1. William Lyon Mackenzie, *Sketches of Canada and the United States* (London, 1833), 89.
2. George Brown, *Building the Canadian Nation* (Toronto: J.M. Dent & Sons, 1958), 531–34.

Chapter 1: In the Beginning

1. Mary Lou Fox, "First Nations Celebrations Throughout the Year," in *My Cultural Handbook* (Willowdale, ON: The Ontario Historical Society, 1995), 7–8.
2. Walter S. Avis, ed., *A Concise Dictionary of Canadianisms* (Toronto: Gage Educational Publishing, 1973), 191.

Notes

Chapter 2: Welcome to the New Year

1. William Sansom, *A Book of Christmas* (Toronto: McGraw-Hill, 1968), 53; and Joan Alcock, "The Festival of Christmas," in *Feasting and Fasting: Proceedings Oxford Symposium on Food and Cookery 1990* (London: Prospect Books, 1991), 28, 32.
2. Caroline Parry, *Let's Celebrate: Canada's Special Days* (Toronto: Kids Can Press, 1987), 54.
3. Joseph Gaer, *Holidays Around the World* (Toronto: McClelland & Stewart, 1953), 140.
4. Elizabeth Russell Papers, quoted in Edith Firth, *The Town of York 1793–1815* (Toronto: University of Toronto Press, 1962), 257–58.
5. Robert Barlow McCrea, *Lost Amid the Fogs: Sketches of Life in Newfoundland, England's Ancient Colony* (London: Sampson, Low, Son and Marston, 1869), 292–97.
6. Dorothy Marsh and Carol Brock, eds., *Good Housekeeping Party Menus and Recipes* (Toronto: The Star Weekly, 1949), 276.

Chapter 3: Sir John A. at Table

1. Lena Newman, *The John A. Macdonald Album* (Montreal: Tundra Books, 1974), 46.
2. Harry Bruce, "Confederation," in *Canada 1812–1871: The Formative Years* (Toronto: Imperial Oil Limited, 1965), 65.
3. *Ibid.*, 66.
4. Hilary Abrahamson, *Victorians at Table: Dining Traditions in Nineteenth-Century Ontario* (Toronto: Ontario Ministry of Culture and Recreation, 1981), 18.
5. Frederic Nicholls and A.W. Wright, compilers, *Report of the Demonstration in Honour of the Fortieth Anniversary of Sir John A. Macdonald's Entrance into Public Life* (Toronto: Canadian Manufacturer Publishing Company, 1885), 18.
6. Ruth Spicer and Marion Elliot, *Christmas Through the Years: New*

Brunswick Recipes and Recollections (St. Stephen, NB: Print 'N' Press Ltd., 1982), 19.

7.   McCord Museum, Montreal, *C285 Collection of Menus 1853–1978.*

Chapter 4: Remembering "Rabbie" Burns

1.   J. Logie Robertson, *The Poetical Works of Robert Burns* (Toronto: Oxford University Press, 1908), 297.

2.   André L. Simon and Robin Howe, *A Dictionary of Gastronomy* (New York: The Overlook Press, 1978).

3.   Robertson, *The Poetical Works of Robert Burns*, 258.

Chapter 5: L'Ordre de bon temps, Order of Good Cheer

1.   For a more detailed description of the search and choice of sites for settlements, see Agnes Maule Machar, "Samuel de Champlain," in *Great Canadians from Cartier to Laurier*, ed. T.G. Marquis (Washington, DC: Library of Congress, 1903), 18–33.

2.   Marc Lescarbot, *The Theatre of Neptune in New France, 1609*, trans. P. Erondelle (New York: Harper and Brothers, 1928), 118.

3.   *Ibid.*, 118.

4.   Marie Nightingale, *Out of Old Nova Scotia Kitchens* (New York: Charles Scribner's Sons, 1971), 92.

5.   *Traditional Recipes of Atlantic Canada: Nova Scotia* #6 (St. John's, NL: Target Marketing, Inc., n.d.), 1.

Chapter 6: St. Valentine and the Foods of Love

1.   Lena Newman, *The John A. Macdonald Album* (Montreal: Tundra Books, 1974), 46–47.

2.   *Canadian Formulas for Good Cookery: All Guaranteed and Tested in the Finest Home Kitchens of Ontario, Vol. 1* (Toronto: Ontario Federation for the Cerebral Palsied, 1984), 4.

3. *Selected Recipes* (Oshawa, ON: W.A. Group, Simcoe Street United Church, 1938), 63. Maraschino is a sweet liqueur with a highly concentrated flavour, first produced over two hundred years ago in Zara, Yugoslavia. It was later produced in Italy also.

4. *Just Desserts* (Toronto: Woman's Association, Group "D," Lawrence Park, Community Church, 1951), 58.

5. E.F. "Ted" Eaton, *Waste Not Want Not: A Booke of Cookery* (Fredericton, NB: Omega Publishing, 1978), 79.

Chapter 7: *Gung Hei Fat Choi*

1. L. Chan-Marples, "Chinese Laundry and Restaurant for 1905 Street, Fort Edmonton Park" (Edmonton: Unpublished research paper, 1983).

2. Denise Helly, *Les Chinois à Montréal* (Quebec City: Institut québécois de research sur la culture, 1987), 19.

3. Dora Nipp, "The Chinese in Toronto," in *Gathering Place: Peoples and Neighbourhoods of Toronto, 1834–1945*, ed. Robert F. Harney (Toronto: Multicultural History Society of Ontario, 1985), 41.

4. Jean R. Burnet, "New Arrivals in the 20th Century and Their Food Traditions," in *Consuming Passions: Eating and Drinking Traditions in Ontario*, eds. Dorothy Duncan and Glenn Lockwood (Willowdale, ON: The Ontario Historical Society, 1990), 256.

5. *Ibid.*, 256.

6. *Ibid.*, 256.

7. Valerie Mah, "Chinese Food Traditions," in *From Cathay to Canada: Chinese Cuisine in Transition*, ed. Jo Marie Powers (Willowdale, ON: The Ontario Historical Society, 1998), 2–3.

8. *Ibid.*, 4–5.

9. Carol Ferguson and Margaret Fraser, *A Century of Canadian Home Cooking: 1900 Through the '90s* (Scarborough, ON: Prentice Hall Canada, 1992), 69. This recipe appeared in many Canadian cookbooks from the beginning of the twentieth century to the present.

Chapter 8: Shrove Tuesday

1. Len Margaret, *Fish and Brewis, Toutens and Tales* (St. Leonard's, NL: Breakwater Books, 1980), 4–5.
2. *Adventures in Cooking* (Vancouver: Evergreen Press, 1958), 131. This book is the Centennial Cook Book of the British Columbia Women's Institutes.

Chapter 9: St. David's Day

1. T. Tusser, *Five Hundreth Pointes of Good Husbandrie ... Newly Augmented*, 1590, quoted in C. Anne Wilson, *Food and Drink in Britain* (Markham, ON: Penguin Canada, 1973), 185.
2. Bobby Freeman, *First Catch Your Peacock: A Book of Welsh Food* (Griffithstown, Wales: Image Imprint, 1980), 34.
3. *Ibid.*, 40–42.
4. *From Our Tables Wrth Ein Bwrdd* (Toronto: Dewi Sant Welsh United Church, 2006), iii.
5. *Ibid.*, 79.
6. André L. Simon and Robin Howe, *Dictionary of Gastronomy* (Woodstock, NY: The Overlook Press, 1978).
7. *Let's Bake Bread!* (Willowdale, ON: The Ontario Historical Society, 1992), 5. With thanks to Jeanne Hughes, daughter of Dorothy Grove.

Chapter 10: Sap's Running!

1. Jonathan Carver, *Three Years Travels Through the Interior Parts of North America* (Philadelphia, 1796), 215.
2. John Ross Robertson, ed., *The Diary of Mrs. John Graves Simcoe* (Toronto: William Briggs, 1911), 219.
3. Joseph Bouchette, *A Topographical Description of the Province of Lower Canada with Remarks upon Upper Canada* (London, 1815), 88.

4. *Manitoba's Heritage Cookery* (Winnipeg: Manitoba Historical Society, 1992), 11.

5. John Lynch, "Report of the State of Agriculture in the County of Grey — 1853," *Journal and Transactions of the Board of Agriculture of Upper Canada, Vol. 1* (Toronto: 1856), quoted in *When the Work's All Done This Fall* (Toronto: Stoddart Publishing, 1989), 183.

6. Andrew Picken, *The Canadas,* 2nd ed. (London: 1836), 201.

7. Andrew Oliver, *A View of Lower Canada Interspersed with Canadian Tales and Anecdotes, and Interesting Information to Intending Emigrants* (Edinburgh, 1821), 91.

8. Micheline Mongrain-Dontigny, *Traditional Quebec Cooking: A Treasure of Heirloom Recipes* (La Tuque, QC: Les Éditions la bonne recette, 1995), 145.

9. E.A. Howes, *With a Glance Backward* (Toronto: Oxford University Press, 1939), quoted in *Pierre and Janet Berton's Canadian Food Guide* (Toronto: McClelland & Stewart, 1974), 22.

Chapter 11: St. Patrick's Day

1. Marie Nightingale, *Out of Old Nova Scotia Kitchens* (Baddeck, NS: Petheric Press, 1978), 16.

2. Lieutenant Governor Archibald of Nova Scotia, speaking at Centennial Celebrations, 1880, in Stewiacke, Nova Scotia, quoted in Nightingale, *Out of Old Nova Scotia Kitchens*, 17.

3. Len Margaret, *Fish and Brewis, Toutens and Tales* (St. Leonard's, NL: Breakwater Books, 1980), 6.

4. L.E.F. English, *Historic Newfoundland and Labrador* (St. John's, NL: Tourism Branch, Department of Development, Province of Newfoundland and Labrador, 1955), 44.

5. Dorothy Marsh and Carol Brock, eds., *Good Housekeeping Party Menus and Recipes* (Toronto: Pyramid Publications, 1958), 43 and 292.

6. Nellie Lyle Pattinson, *Canadian Cook Book* (Toronto: Ryerson Press, 1923), 203.

7. Dorothy Marsh and Carol Brock, eds., *Good Housekeeping Party Menus and Recipes* (Toronto: *The Star Weekly*, 1949), 143.

8. *St. Barnabas' Church Liturgical Year Cook Book* (Medicine Hat, AB: St. Barnabas' Anglican Church, 1974), 53.

9. Private family collection.

Chapter 12: Celebrations of Survival

1. Sheldon and Judith Godfrey, *Burn This Gossip: The True Story of George Benjamin of Belleville, Canada's First Jewish Member of Parliament 1857–1863* (Toronto: The Duke and George Press, 1991), 34.

2. Jean R. Burnet with Howard Palmer, *"Coming Canadians": An Introduction to a History of Canada's Peoples* (Toronto: McClelland & Stewart, 1988), 13–14, 16.

3. G.P. (Glyn) Allen, *Days to Remember* (Toronto: Ontario Ministry of Culture and Recreation, 1979), 57–59.

4. Judith Hoffman Corwin, *Jewish Holiday Fun* (New York: Julian Messner, 1987), 46–47.

5. *St. Barnabas' Church Liturgical Year Cook Book* (Medicine Hat, AB: St. Barnabas' Anglican Church, 1974), 145.

6. *Manitoba's Heritage Cookery* (Winnipeg: Manitoba Historical Society, 1992), 84, 85.

Chapter 13: God's Day

1. Kay and Marshall Lee, eds., *The Illuminated Book of Days* (New York: G.P. Putnam's Sons., 1979), 33.

2. Nellie Lyle Pattinson, *Canadian Cook Book* (Toronto: Ryerson Press, 1923), 280.

Chapter 14: He Is Risen!

1. John Lambert, "French Canadian Characters and Customs" (1806–08),

quoted in *Early Travellers in the Canadas*, ed. Gerald M. Craig (Toronto: Macmillan Company of Canada, 1955), 28.

2.   *Elora Observer and Center Wellington Times*, March 29, 1877, 2.

3.   John H. Young, *Our Deportment; or the Manners, Conduct and Dress of the Most Refined Society* (Paris, ON: John S. Brown, 1883), 66.

4.   Barbara Parry, "An Easter to Remember," in *Farmers' Advocate and Canadian Countrymen*, March 28, 1953, 17.

5.   Katherine C. Lewis Flynn, *Mrs. Flynn's Cookbook* (Charlottetown: Ladies of St. Elizabeth's and Society in Aid of St. Vincent's Orphanage, 1931), 4.

Chapter 15: "Damned Cold Water Drinking Societies!"

1.   Frances Stewart, *Our Forest Home*, 2nd ed. (Montreal Gazette Printing and Publishing Company, 1902), 174–76.

2.   Patrick Shirreff, *A Tour Through North America* (Edinburgh: Oliver and Boyd, 1835), 125.

3.   Susanna Moodie, *Roughing It in the Bush* (Toronto: McClelland & Stewart, reprint of original, 1852), 305.

4.   Joseph Pickering, *Inquiries of an Emigrant* (London, 4th ed., 1832), 72.

5.   Craig Heron, *BOOZE* (Toronto: Between the Lines, 2003), 32.

6.   Reminiscences of David Dobie, quoted in W.L. Smith, *The Pioneers of Old Ontario* (Toronto: G.N. Morang, 1923), 223–24; and Edwin Guillet, *Pioneer Days in Upper Canada* (Toronto: University of Toronto Press, 1933), 134.

7.   Heron, *BOOZE*, 53, 399.

8.   Reverend M.A. Garland and J.J. Talman, "Pioneer Drinking Habits and the Rise of the Temperance Agitation in Upper Canada Prior to 1840," in *Papers and Records, Vol. XXVII* (Toronto: The Ontario Historical Society, 1931), 353–54.

9.   C.O. Ermatinger, *Talbot Regime* (St. Thomas, ON: Municipal World, 1914), 167.

10. Ruth Elizabeth Spence, *Prohibition in Canada* (Toronto: Ontario Branch of the Dominion Alliance, 1919), 46.

11. *Ibid.*, 49–51, 64.
12. Anna Jameson, *Winter Studies and Summer Rambles in Canada* (London, 1838), 84.
13. Mary Grey Lundy Duncan, *America As I Found It* (New York: R. Carter, 1852), 194–95.
14. John Howison, *Sketches of Upper Canada Domestic, Local and Characteristic* (Edinburgh: Oliver and Boyd, 1821), 118.
15. Colonel Francis Hall, *Travels in Canada and the United States* (London: Longman, Hurst, Reese, Orme & Brown, 1818), 213.
16. Moodie, *Roughing It in the Bush*, 64.
17. Edwin Guillet, *Pioneer Inns and Taverns Vol III.* (Toronto: Ontario Publishing Company, 1958), 180.

Chapter 16: Mother

1. Judith Drynan, "Simnel Cake Part of Mothering Sunday," *Globe and Mail*, March 5, 1986, E2.
2. Kate Aitken, *Kate Aitken's Canadian Cook Book* (Toronto: The Star Weekly, 1949), 294, 297–98.
3. G.P. (Glyn) Allen, *Days to Remember* (Toronto: Ontario Ministry of Culture and Recreation, 1979), 10.
4. Marjorie Elwood, "Mother-Daughter Tea," *The Star Weekly*, October 3 1953, 10.
5. Esther Baldwin York, "Heroine of the Hearthfire," in *Mother's Day Greetings*, ed. van b. booper (Milwaukee, WI: Ideals Publishing Co. 1958), 36.

Chapter 17: Happy Birthday, Queen Victoria

1. Jill Foran, *Victoria Day* (Calgary: Weigl Educational Publishers, 2003), 16; and Caroline Parry, *Let's Celebrate!* (Toronto: Kids Can Press, 1987), 140.
2. Lucy Booth Martyn, *The Face of Early Toronto: An Archival Record 1797–1936* (Sutton West, ON: Paget Press, 1982), 16.

3. *Ibid.*, 17.
4. J.B. Priestley, *Victoria's Heyday* (Harmondsworth, Eng.: Penguin Books, 1974), 23.
5. *Ibid.*, 25.
6. Jan Reid and Maite Manjon, *The Great British Breakfast* (London: Michael Joseph, 1981).
7. *Fredericton Cathedral Memorial Hall Cookery Book* (1920), 54.

Chapter 18: La Fête de St-Jean-Baptiste

1. Ruth Manning-Sanders, *Festivals* (London: Cox & Wyman, 1972), 98.
2. *Ibid.*, 99.
3. Florence Berger, *Cooking for Christ* (Des Moines, IA: National Catholic Rural Life Conference, 1949), 91–92.
4. Interview with Diabo, Kahnawke, Mohawk Territory, Quebec, May 29, 2010.
5. Jehane Benoit, *Madame Benoit's Library of Cooking Vol. II* (Montreal: Les Messageries du St-Laurent, 1972), 1000.
6. *The Five Roses Cook Book* (Montreal: Lake of the Woods Milling Company, 1915), 131, 133.
7. *From Saskatchewan Homemakers' Kitchens* (Saskatoon: Saskatchewan Homemaker's Clubs, 1955), 305.
8. *Manitoba's Heritage Cookery* (Winnipeg: Manitoba Historical Society, 1992), 149.

Chapter 19: Dominion Day

1. George W. Brown, *Building the Canadian Nation* (Toronto: J.M. Dent & Sons, 1958), 399.
2. Lena Newman, *The John A. Macdonald Album* (Montreal: Tundra Books 1974), 76.
3. *Toronto Leader*, July 3, 1867, quoted in Pierre and Janet Berton, *Pierre*

and Janet Berton's Canadian Food Guide (Toronto: McClelland & Stewart, 1974), 52.

4.   Nellie Lyle Pattinson, *Canadian Cook Book* (Toronto: Ryerson Press 1923), 29–30.

5.   Berton, *Pierre and Janet Berton's Canadian Food Guide*, 67.

.Chapter 20: Feasts of the Fur Traders

1.   Florida Town, *The North West Company: Frontier Merchants* (Toronto: Umbrella Press, 1999), 12.

2.   W.S. Wallace, "Fort William of the Fur Trade," *The Beaver* (December 1949), 16; and *Fort William: Hinge of a Nation*, feasibility study prepared by National Heritage, Ltd., for the Province of Ontario, 36.

3.   Leslie F. Harman, *Forts of Canada* (Toronto: McClelland & Stewart, 1969), 205.

4.   *Ibid.*, 209.

5.   Grace Lee Nute, *The Voyageurs' Highway* (St. Paul, MN: Minnesota Historical Society, 1951), 54.

6.   Harman, *Forts of Canada*, 205.

7.   *Ibid.*, 205.

8.   "The Oregon Territory," *The Builder*, 1844, Vol. II, 9.

9.   *The North West Company, from Lachine to Grand Portage: The North West Indian Trade* (Cornwall, ON: Inverarden Regency Cottage Museum, 1993).

10.   L.V. Burpee, "The Beaver Club," *History Society Report* (1924), 73–92.

11.   Marjorie Wilkins Campbell, *McGillivray, Lord of the Northwest* (Toronto: Clarke, Irwin, 1962), 93.

12.   Burpee "The Beaver Club," 73–92.

13.   Harman, *Forts of Canada*, 215.

14.   A.A. Chesterfield, "New Year's in the Far North," *Montreal Daily Star*, December, 31, 1910, 20, quoted in William C. James, *A Fur Trader's Photographs* (Montreal and Kingston: McGill-Queen's University Press, 1985), 14.

Notes

Chapter 20: Pic-Nics, Pleasure Parties, and Garden Parties

1. Joseph Willcocks, *Memorandum and Letter Book*, Library and Archives Canada, quoted in Edith Firth, *The Town of York 1793–1815* (Toronto: University of Toronto Press, 1962), 232.
2. Lena Newman, *The John A. Macdonald Album* (Montreal: Tundra Books, 1974), 152–53.
3. Juliette Elkon and Elaine Ross, *Menus for Entertaining* (New York: Hastings House Publishers, 1960), 22–23. Two American visitors remember a garden party at Buckingham Palace, circa 1930.
4. Pat McClennan, *Ladies Please Provide* (Centennial Committee 1967 Cedar Grove Community Club), 19.

Chapter 22: Secret Societies

1. *REDBRICK* (Vankleek Hill, ON: Vankleek Hill and District Historical Society, 2001), 2.
2. Richard Merritt, Nancy Butler, and Michael Power, *The Capital Years* (Toronto: Dundurn Press, 1991), 199.
3. Kate Aitken, *Never a Day So Bright* (Toronto: Longmans Green & Co., 1956), 141–42.
4. *Ibid.*, 139–40.
5. The York Pioneer and Historical Society, Toronto.

Chapter 23: The High Holy Days

1. Sheldon and Judith Godfrey, *Burn This Gossip: The True Story of George Benjamin of Belleville, Canada's First Jewish Member of Parliament 1857–1863* (Toronto: The Duke and George Press, 1991), various pages, including 34–35.
2. *Ibid.*, 2.
3. *Ibid.*, 66.
4. Sondra Gotlieb, *Cross Canada Cooking* (Saanichton, BC: Hancock

House, 1976), 135.

5. Bonnie Stern, "Have a Sweet Delicious New Year," *Toronto Star*, September 24, 1997, F3.

6. *Manitoba's Heritage Cookery* (Winnipeg: Manitoba Historical Society, 1992), 84.

Chapter 24: Labour Day

1. Edith G. Firth, ed., *The Town of York 1815–1834* (Toronto: The Champlain Society, 1966), 36.

2. *Ibid.*, 39.

3. *Ibid.*, 41.

4. Janice Acton, Penny Goldsmith, Bonnie Shepard, eds., *Women at Work 1850–1930* (Toronto: Canadian Women's Educational Press, 1974), 27.

5. Firth, *The Town of York*, 78.

6. Steve Murray, "What Exactly Is Labour Day?" *National Post*, Toronto, August 31, 2007, PM12.

7. Desmond Morton, "The Same Views, 100 Labour Days Later," *Toronto Star*, September 1, 1986, A9.

Chapter 25: Let Us Give Thanks

1. Richard Hakluyt, *The Principall Navigations, Voiages and Discoveries of the English Nation* (London: George Bishop and Ralph Newberie, 1589), reprinted from the first edition of Hakluyt's *Voyages* by Rear Admiral Richard Collinson (New York: Hakluyt Society, 1987), 252.

2. *A Collage of Canadian Cooking* (Ottawa: Canadian Home Economics Association, 1979); and St. Barnabas' Church Liturgical Year Cook Book (Medicine Hat, AB: St. Barnabas' Anglican Church, 1974), 129.

Notes

Chapter 26: All Hallows' Eve, All Saints' Day, and All Souls' Day

1. Florence Berger, *Cooking for Christ* (Des Moines, IA: National Catholic Rural Life Conference, 1945), 118.

2. Len Margaret, *Fish and Brewis, Toutens and Tales* (St. Leonard's, NL: Breakwater Books, 1980), 100.

3. Dorothy Marsh and Carol Brock, eds., *Good Housekeeping Party Menus and Recipes* (Toronto: Pyramid Publications, 1958), 179, 180, 293.

Chapter 27: Remember, Remember the Fifth of November

1. *The United States and Canada as Seen by Two Brothers in 1858 and 1861* (London, 1862), quoted in Gerald M. Craig, *Early Travellers in the Canadas 1791–1867* (Toronto: Macmillan Company of Canada, 1955), 252.

2. I. Tenen, *This England, Part II* (London: Macmillan, 1962), 149–50.

3. I am grateful to Mary Simonds, who grew up in the Lake District of England and now lives in Whitby, Ontario; Lynne Jeffrey and Ruth Keene, who grew up in the suburbs of London, England, and now live in Toronto and Willowdale, Ontario, respectively; and Jeanne Hughes, who grew up in Wales and now lives in Richmond Hill, Ontario, for sharing their memories with me in March 2010.

4. Thanks to Ruth Keene for sharing that fascinating story on March 11, 2010.

5. Gail Alice Collins, "Remember, Remember the Fifth of November," *Globe and Mail*, November 4, 2005, A18.

6. Keith Penny, who grew up in Newfoundland and now lives in Dunnville, Ontario, shared his memories on March 23, 2010.

7. Interview with Winston Vokey of Bell Island, Newfoundland, who now lives in Barrie, Ontario, March 29, 2010.

Chapter 28: Lest We Forget

1. Anishnawbe Health Toronto, "Feasts and Giveaways," accessed at *www.aht.ca/feasts-and-giveaways* on January 5, 2010.
2. Marie Nightingale, *Out of Old Nova Scotia Kitchens* (New York: Charles Scribner's Sons, 1971), 11.
3. J.O. Swahn, *The Lore of Spices* (London: Senate Publishing, 1991), 124, 130.
4. Carol Petch, *Old Hemmingford Recipes* (Hemmingford, QC: Imprimie Cyan Printing, 1977), 73.
5. *Manitoba's Heritage Cookery* (Winnipeg: Manitoba Historical Society, 1992), 167.
6. Valerie Mah, "Chinese Food Traditions," in *From Cathay to Canada: Chinese Food in Transition* (Willowdale, ON: The Ontario Historical Society, 1998), 8.

Chapter 29: La Tire Ste-Catherine

1. Marie Nightingale, *Out of Old Nova Scotia Kitchens* (New York: Charles Scribner's Sons, 1971), 192.
2. Micheline Mongrain-Dontigny, *Traditional Quebec Cooking* (La Tuque, QC: Les Éditions la bonne recettes, 1995), 134.
3. Walter S. Avis, ed., *A Concise Dictionary of Canadianisms* (Toronto: Gage Educational, 1973), 46, 225.

Chapter 30: St. Andrew

1. Mistress Margaret Dods, *Cook and Housewife's Manual: A Practical System of Modern Domestic Cookery and Family Management* (Edinburgh: Oliver and Boyd, 1829), 69.
2. McCord Museum, Montreal, *C285 Collection of Menus 1853–1978*.
3. "The Nicht 1896," *Newsletter of the St. Andrew's Society of Toronto*, 2007, No.1, 5.

Notes

Chapter 31: Feast of Dedication

1. *Manitoba's Heritage Cookery* (Winnipeg: Manitoba Historical Society, 1992), 83.
2. Bonnie Stern, "Lighten Up During Festival of Lights," *Toronto Star*, November 23, 1994, F7.

Chapter 32: Christ's Mass

1. Caroline Parry, *Let's Celebrate!* (Toronto: Kids Can Press, 1987), 26; and Kay and Marshall Lee, eds., *The Illuminated Book of Days* (Toronto: Longmans Canada, 1979), 182.
2. Norman E. Ross, ed., *The Pageantry of Christmas Vol. Two* (New York: Time Incorporated, 1963), 74.
3. André Pechat, "Our First Christmas Tree," *The Beaver* (April/May 1997), 46.
4. *It's Time for Christmas* (Philadelphia: Macrae Smith Company, 1959), 111–12.
5. Parry, *Let's Celebrate!* 28.
6. *Manitoba's Heritage Cookery* (Winnipeg: Manitoba Historical Society, 1992), 140.
7. *Report of the Royal Commission on Chinese Immigration, 1885* (Ottawa: Royal Commission on Chinese Immigrants, 1885); and E. Wickberg, *From China to Canada* (Toronto: McClelland & Stewart, 1982), 155.
8. Julie V. Watson, *Favourite Recipes from Old Prince Edward Island Kitchens* (Willowdale, ON: Hounslow Press, 1986), 334.
9. Ivan F. Jesperson, *Fat-Back and Molasses* (St. John's, NL: Reverend Ivan F. Jesperson, 1974), 88.
10. Len Margaret, *Fish and Brewis, Toutens and Tales* (St. Leonard's, NL: Breakwater Books, 1980), 38.
11. Florence R. Harvey, *Pioneering on the C.P.R.* (Sudbury, ON: Sudbury District Branch of the Ontario Genealogical Society, 2009). A historical reprint of the original manuscript by Florence Howey, 1936, 54–55.

Chapter 33: Season of Celebrations

1. Richard Merritt, Nancy Butler, and Michael Power, eds., *The Capital Years* (Toronto: Dundurn Press, 1991), 199, 219.
2. Interviews with Josie and Keith Penny formerly of Newfoundland and Labrador, who now live in Dunnville, Ontario, March 23, 2010; and interviews with Inez and Winston Vokey, formerly of Bell Island, Newfoundland, who now lives in Barrie, Ontario, March 29, 2010.
3. Kay and Marshall Lee, eds., *The Illuminated Book of Days* (Toronto: Longmans Canada, 1979), 183.
4. Barb Holland, "Fare Exchange," *Toronto Star*, April 8, 1992, D9. Recipe submitted by Liz Richmond of Paris, Ontario.
5. André L. Simon and Robin Howe. *A Dictionary of Gastronomy* (New York: The Overlook Press, 1978).

Chapter 34: New Year's Eve and Hogmanay

1. The Ingonish Women's Hospital Auxiliary, *From the Highlands and the Sea* (Halifax, NS: McCurdy Printing and Typesetting Limited, 1984), 39.

Bibliography

Abrahamson, Hilary. *Victorians at Table: Dining Traditions in Nineteenth Century Ontario*. Toronto: Ontario Ministry of Culture and Recreation, 1981.

Acton, Janice, and Penny Goldsmith and Bonnie Shepard, eds. *Women at Work 1850–1930*. Toronto: Canadian Women's Educational Press, 1974.

Adventures in Cooking. Vancouver: Evergreen Press, 1958.

Aitken, Kate. *Kate Aitken's Canadian Cook Book*. Toronto: The Star Weekly, 1949.

____. *Never a Day So Bright*. Toronto: Longmans Green, 1956.

Alcock, Joan. "The Festival of Christmas," *Feasting and Fasting: Proceedings Oxford Symposium on Food and Cookery, 1990*. London: Prospect Books, 1991.

Allen, G.P. (Glyn). *Days to Remember*. Toronto: Ontario Ministry of Culture and Recreation, 1979.

Anishnawbe Health Toronto. *Feasts and Giveaways*, accessed at *www.aht.ca/feasts-and-giveaways* on January 5, 2010.

Avis, Walter S., ed. *A Concise Dictionary of Canadianisms*. Toronto: Gage Educational Publishing, 1973.

Benoit, Jehane. *Madame Benoit's Library of Cooking Vols. 1–12.* Montreal: Les Messageries du St-Laurent, 1972.

Berger, Florence. *Cooking for Christ.* Des Moines, IA: National Catholic Rural Life Conference, 1945.

Berton, Pierre, and Janet Berton. *Pierre and Janet Berton's Canadian Food Guide.* Toronto: McClelland & Stewart, 1974.

Bouchette, Joseph. *A Topographical Description of the Province of Lower Canada with Remarks upon Upper Canada.* London, 1815.

Brown, George. *Building the Canadian Nation.* Toronto: J.M. Dent & Sons, 1958.

Bruce, Harry. "Confederation," in *Canada 1812–1871: The Formative Years.* Toronto: Imperial Oil Limited, 1965.

Burnet, Jean R. "New Arrivals in the 20th Century and Their Food Traditions," in *Consuming Passions: Eating and Drinking Traditions in Ontario.* Eds. Dorothy Duncan and Glenn Lockwood. Willowdale, ON: The Ontario Historical Society, 1990.

Burnet, Jean R., and Howard Palmer. *"Coming Canadians": An Introduction to a History of Canada's Peoples.* Toronto: McClelland & Stewart, 1988.

Burpee, L.V. "The Beaver Club," *History Society Report* (1924).

Campbell, Marjorie Wilkins. *McGillivray, Lord of the Northwest.* Toronto: Clarke, Irwin, 1962.

Canadian Formulas for Good Cookery: All Guaranteed and Tested in the Finest Home Kitchens of Ontario, Vol. 1. Toronto: Ontario Federation for the Cerebral Palsied, 1984.

Carver, Jonathan. *Three Years Travels Through the Interior Parts of North America.* Philadelphia, 1796.

Chan-Marples, L. "Chinese Laundry and Restaurant for 1905 Street, Fort Edmonton Park." Edmonton: Unpublished research paper, 1983.

Chesterfield, A.A. "New Year's in the Far North," *Montreal Daily Star*, December 31, 1910.

A Collage of Canadian Cooking. Ottawa: Canadian Home Economics Association, 1979.

Bibliography

Collins, Gail Alice. "Remember, Remember the Fifth of November," *Globe and Mail*, November 4, 2005.

Collinson, Rear Admiral Richard. *Voyages*. New York: Hakluyt Society, 1987.

Cooke, Maude C. *Social Etiquette or Manners and Customs in Polite Society*. Toronto: J.L. Nichols & Co, 1896.

Corwin, Judith Hoffman. *Jewish Holiday Fun*. New York: Julian Messner, 1987.

Craig, Gerald M. *Early Travellers in the Canadas 1791–1867*. Toronto: Macmillan Company of Canada, 1955.

Dods, Mistress Margaret. *Cook and Housewife's Manual: A Practical System of Modern Domestic Cookery and Family Management*. Edinburgh: Oliver and Boyd, 1829.

Drynan, Judith. "Simnel Cake Part of Mothering Sunday," *Globe and Mail*, March 5, 1986.

Duncan, Dorothy. *Canadians at Table: Food, Fellowship and Folklore, a Culinary History of Canada*. Toronto: Dundurn Press, 2006.

____. *Nothing More Comforting: Canada's Heritage Food*. Toronto: Dundurn Press, 2003.

Duncan, Mary Grey Lundy. *America As I Found It*. New York: R. Carter, 1852.

Eaton, E.F. "Ted." *Waste Not Want Not: A Booke of Cookery*. Fredericton, NB: Omega Publishing, 1978.

Elkon, Juliette, and Elaine Ross. *Menus for Entertaining*. New York: Hastings House Publishers, 1960.

Elora Observer and Center Wellington Times, March 29, 1877.

Elwood, Marjorie. "Mother-Daughter Tea," *The Star Weekly*, October 3, 1953.

English, L.E.F. *Historic Newfoundland and Labrador*. St. Johns, NL: Tourism Branch, Department of Development, Province of Newfoundland and Labrador, 1955.

Ermatinger, C.O. *Talbot Regime*. St. Thomas, ON: Municipal World, 1914.

Ferguson, Carol, and Margaret Fraser. *A Century of Canadian Home Cooking: 1900 Through the '90s*. Scarborough, ON: Prentice Hall Canada, 1992.

Firth, Edith. *The Town of York 1793–1815*. Toronto: University of Toronto Press, 1962.

The Five Roses Cook Book. Montreal: Lake of the Woods Milling Company, 1915.

Flynn, Katherine C. Lewis. *Mrs. Flynn's Cookbook*. Charlottetown: Ladies of St. Elizabeth's and Society in Aid of St. Vincent's Orphanage, 1931.

Foran, Jill. *Victoria Day*. Calgary: Weigl Educational Publishers, 2003.

Fort William: Hinge of a Nation. Feasibility study prepared by National Heritage, Ltd., for the Province of Ontario.

Fox, Mary Lou. "First Nations Celebrations Throughout the Year," *My Cultural Handbook*. Willowdale, ON: The Ontario Historical Society, 1995.

Fredericton Cathedral Memorial Hall Cookery Book. 1920.

Freeman, Bobby. *First Catch Your Peacock: A Book of Welsh Food*. Griffithstown, Wales: Image Imprint, 1980.

From Our Tables Wrth Ein Bwrdd. Toronto: Dewi Sant Welsh United Church, 2006.

From Saskatchewan Homemakers' Kitchens. Saskatoon: Saskatchewan Homemakers' Clubs, 1955.

Gaer, Joseph. *Holidays Around the World*. Toronto: McClelland & Stewart, 1953.

Garland, Reverend M.A., and J.J. Talman. "Pioneer Drinking Habits and the Rise of the Temperance Agitation in Upper Canada Prior to 1840," *Papers and Records, Vol. XXVII*. Toronto: The Ontario Historical Society, 1931.

Godfrey, Sheldon, and Judith Godfrey. *Burn This Gossip: The True Story of George Benjamin of Belleville, Canada's First Jewish Member of Parliament 1857–1863*. Toronto: The Duke and George Press, 1991.

Gotlieb, Sondra. *Cross Canada Cooking*. Saanichton, BC: Hancock House, 1976.

Gourse, Leslie. *Native American Courtship and Marriage*. Summertown, TN: Native Voices, 2005.

Guillet, Edwin. *Pioneer Days in Upper Canada*. Toronto: University of Toronto Press, 1933.

Bibliography

_____. *Pioneer Inns and Taverns Vol III.* Toronto: Ontario Publishing Company, 1958.

Hakluyt, Richard. *The Principle Navigation, Voiages and Discoveries of the English Nation.* London: George Bishop and Ralph Newberie, 1589.

Hall, Colonel Francis. *Travels in Canada and the United States.* London: Longman, Hurst, Reese, Orme & Brown, 1818.

Harman, Leslie F. *Forts of Canada.* Toronto: McClelland & Stewart, 1969.

Harvey, Florence R. *Pioneering on the C.P.R.* Sudbury, ON: Sudbury District Branch of the Ontario Genealogical Society, 2009.

Helly, Denise. *Les Chinois à Montréal.* Quebec City: Institut québécois de research sur la culture, 1987.

Heron, Craig. *BOOZE.* Toronto: Between the Lines, 2003.

Holland, Barb. "Fare Exchange," *Toronto Star*, April 8, 1992.

Howes, E.A. *With a Glance Backward.* Toronto: Oxford University Press, 1939.

Howison, John. *Sketches of Upper Canada Domestic, Local and Characteristic.* Edinburgh: Oliver and Boyd, 1821.

Ingonish Women's Hospital Auxiliary. *From the Highlands and the Sea.* Halifax, NS: McCurdy Printing and Typesetting, 1984.

It's Time for Christmas. Philadelphia: Macrae Smith Company, 1959.

James, William C. *A Fur Trader's Photographs.* Montreal and Kingston: McGill-Queen's University Press, 1985.

Jamieson, Anna. *Winter Studies and Summer Rambles in Canada.* London, 1838.

Jesperson, Ivan F. *Fat-Back and Molasses.* St. John's, NL: Reverend Ivan F. Jesperson, 1974.

Just Desserts. Toronto: Woman's Association, Group "D," Lawrence Park, Community Church, 1951.

Lee, Kay, and Marshall Lee. *The Illuminated Book of Days.* New York: G.P. Putnam's Sons, 1979.

Lescarbot, Marc. *The Theatre of Neptune in New France, 1609.* Trans. P. Erondelle. New York: Harper and Brothers, 1928.

Let's Bake Bread! Willowdale, ON: The Ontario Historical Society, 1992.

Lynch, John. "Report of the State of Agriculture in the County of Grey — 1853," in *Journal and Transactions of the Board of Agriculture of Upper Canada, Vol. 1* (Toronto, 1856).

Machar, Agnes Maule. "Samuel de Champlain," in *Great Canadians from Cartier to Laurier*, ed. T.G. Marquis. Washington, DC: Library of Congress, 1903.

Mackenzie, William Lyon. *Sketches of Canada and the United States.* London, 1833.

Mah, Valerie. "Chinese Food Traditions," in *From Cathay to Canada: Chinese Cuisine in Transition*. Ed. Jo Marie Powers. Willowdale, ON: The Ontario Historical Society, 1998.

Manitoba's Heritage Cookery. Winnipeg: Manitoba Historical Society, 1992.

Manning-Sanders, Ruth. *Festivals.* London: Cox & Wyman, 1972.

Margaret, Len. *Fish and Brewis, Toutens and Tales.* St. Leonard's, NL: Breakwater Books, 1980.

Marsh, Dorothy, and Carol Brock, eds. *Good Housekeeping Party Menus and Recipes.* Toronto: The Star Weekly, 1949.

Martyn, Lucy Booth. *The Face of Early Toronto: An Archival Record 1797–1936.* Sutton West, ON: Paget Press, 1982.

McClennan, Pat. *Ladies Please Provide.* Centennial Committee 1967 Cedar Grove Community Club.

McCord Museum, Montreal, *Collection of Menus 1853–1978.*

McCrea, Robert Barlow. *Lost Amid the Fogs: Sketches of Life in Newfoundland, England's Ancient Colony.* London: Sampson, Low, Son and Marston, 1869.

McIntosh, David. *When the Work's All Done This Fall.* Toronto: Stoddart Publishing, 1989.

Merritt, Richard, and Nancy Butler and Michael Power, eds. *The Capital Years.* Toronto: Dundurn Press, 1991.

Métis Cookbook and Guide to Healthy Living. Ottawa: Métis Centre, National Aboriginal Health Organization, 2008.

Mongrain-Dontigny, Micheline. *Traditional Quebec Cooking; A Treasure of Heirloom Recipes.* La Tuque, QC: Les Éditions la bonne recette, 1995.

Bibliography

Moodie, Susanna. *Roughing It in the Bush*. Toronto: McClelland & Stewart. Reprint of original, 1852.

Morton, Desmond, "The Same Views, 100 Labour Days Later," *Toronto Star*, September 1, 1986.

Murray, Steve. "What Exactly Is Labour Day?" *National Post*, August 31, 2007.

Myers, Lisa, ed. *This Food Is Good for You*. Victoria Harbour, ON: Enaatig Healing Lodge and Learning Centre, 2007.

Newman, Lena. *The John A. Macdonald Album*. Montreal: Tundra Books, 1974.

"The Nicht 1896." *Newsletter of the St. Andrew's Society of Toronto*, 2007, No. 1.

Nightingale, Marie. *Out of Old Nova Scotia Kitchens*. New York: Charles Scribner's Sons, 1971, and Baddeck, NS: Petheric Press, 1978.

Nipp, Dora. "The Chinese in Toronto," in *Gathering Place: Peoples and Neighbourhoods of Toronto, 1834–1945*. Ed. Robert F. Harney. Toronto: Multicultural History Society of Ontario, 1985.

The North West Company, from Lachine to Grand Portage: The North West Indian Trade. Cornwall, ON: Inverarden Regency Cottage Museum, 1993.

Nute, Grace Lee. *The Voyageurs' Highway*. St. Paul, MN: Minnesota Historical Society, 1951.

Oliver, Andrew. *A View of Lower Canada Interspersed with Canadian Tales and Anecdotes, and Interesting Information to Intending Emigrants*. Edinburgh, 1821.

"The Oregon Territory," *The Builder*, 1844, Vol. II, No. 9.

Parry, Barbara. "An Easter to Remember," *Farmers' Advocate and Canadian Countryman*, March 28, 1953.

Parry, Caroline. *Let's Celebrate: Canada's Special Days*. Toronto: Kids Can Press, 1987.

Pattinson, Nellie Lyle. *Canadian Cook Book*. Toronto: Ryerson Press, 1923.

Pechat, André. "Our First Christmas Tree," *The Beaver* (April/May 1997).

Petch, Carol. *Old Hemmingford Recipes*. Hemmingford, QC: Imprimie Cyan Printing, 1977.

Picken, Andrew. *The Canadas*. 2nd ed. London, 1836.

Pickering, Joseph. *Inquiries of an Emigrant*. 4th ed. London, 1832.

Powers, Jo Marie, and Anita Stewart, eds. *Northern Bounty: A Celebration of Canadian Cuisine*. Toronto: Random House of Canada, 1995.

Priestley, J.B. *Victoria's Heyday*. Harmondsworth, Eng.: Penguin Books, 1974.

REDBRICK. Vankleek Hill, ON: Vankleek Hill and District Historical Society, 2001.

Reid, Jan, and Maite Manjon. *The Great British Breakfast*. London: Michael Joseph, 1981.

Report of the Royal Commission on Chinese Immigration, 1885. Ottawa: Royal Commission on Chinese Immigrants, 1885.

Robertson, J. Logie. *The Poetical Works of Robert Burns*. Toronto: Oxford University Press, 1908.

Robertson, John Ross, ed. *The Diary of Mrs. John Graves Simcoe*. Toronto: William Briggs, 1911.

Ross, Norman E. ed. *The Pageantry of Christmas Vol. Two*. New York: Time Incorporated, 1963.

Sansom, William. *A Book of Christmas*. Toronto: McGraw Hill, 1968.

Selected Recipes. Oshawa, ON: W.A. Group, Simcoe Street United Church, 1938.

Shirreff, Patrick. *A Tour Through North America*. Edinburgh: Oliver and Boyd, 1835.

Simon, André L., and Robin Howe. *A Dictionary of Gastronomy*. New York: The Overlook Press, 1978.

Smith, W.L. *Pioneers of Old Ontario*. Toronto: George N. Morang, 1923.

Spence, Ruth Elizabeth. *Prohibition in Canada*. Toronto: Ontario Branch of the Dominion Alliance, 1919.

Spicer, Ruth, and Marion Elliot. *Christmas Through the Years: New Brunswick Recipes and Recollections*. St. Stephen, NB: Print 'N' Press Ltd., 1982.

St. Barnabas' Church Liturgical Year Cook Book. Medicine Hat, AB: St. Barnabas Anglican Church, 1974.

St. Clair, James O., and Yvonne C. LeVert. *Nancy's Wedding Feast and other Tasty Tales*. Sydney, NS: Cape Breton University Press, 2007.

Bibliography

Stern, Bonnie. "Have a Sweet Delicious New Year," *Toronto Star*, September 24, 1997.

____. "Lighten Up During Festival of Lights," *Toronto Star*, November 23, 1994.

Stewart, Frances. *Our Forest Home*. 2nd ed. Montreal: Gazette Printing and Publishing, 1902.

Swahn, J.O. *The Lore of Spices*. London: Senate Publishing Ltd., 1991.

Tenen, I. *This England, Part II*. London: Macmillan, 1962.

Toronto Leader, July 3, 1867.

Town, Florida. *The North West Company: Frontier Merchants*. Toronto: Umbrella Press, 1999.

Traditional Recipes of Atlantic Canada: #1–12. St. John's, NL: Target Marketing, Inc., n.d.

The United States and Canada as Seen by Two Brothers in 1858 and 1861. London, 1862.

Wallace, W.S. "Fort William of the Fur Trade," *The Beaver* (December 1949).

Watson, Julie V. *Favourite Recipes from Old Prince Edward Island Kitchens*. Willowdale, ON: Hounslow Press, 1986.

Wickberg, E. *From China to Canada*. Toronto: McClelland & Stewart, 1982.

Willcocks, Joseph. *Memorandum and Letter Book*. Ottawa: Library and Archives Canada.

Wilson, C. Anne. *Food and Drink in Britain*. Markham, ON: Penguin Books Canada, 1973.

York, Esther Baldwin. "Heroine of the Hearthfire," in *Mother's Day Greetings*. Ed. van b. booper. Milwaukee, WI: Ideals Publishing Co., 1958.

Young, John H. *Our Deportment; or the Manners, Conduct and Dress of the Most Refined Society*. Paris, ON: John S. Brown, 1883.

Index

Index

Index

Index

Index

Index